The Healing Path

The Healing Path

A Guide for Women
Rebuilding Their Lives
After Sexual Abuse

Connie, Marilyn, Brenda, Sharon, Diane, and Caroline

with *John P. Splinter*

OLIVER
NELSON

THOMAS NELSON PUBLISHERS
Nashville

Published in Nashville, Tennessee, by Oliver-Nelson Books, a division of Thomas Nelson, Inc., Publishers, and distributed in Canada by Word Communications, Ltd., Richmond, British Columbia.

Scripture quotations noted NKJV are from THE NEW KING JAMES VERSION. Copyright © 1979, 1980, 1982, Thomas Nelson, Inc., Publishers. Scripture quotations noted RSV are from the Revised Standard Version of the Bible, copyrighted 1946, 1952, © 1971, 1973 by the Division of Christian Education of the National Council of the Churches of Christ in the U.S.A. and used by permission. Scripture quotations noted PHILLIPS are from J. B. Phillips: THE NEW TESTAMENT IN MODERN ENGLISH, Revised Edition. © J. B. Phillips 1958, 1960, 1972. Used by permission of Macmillan Publishing Co., Inc. Scripture quotations marked NIV are taken from the HOLY BIBLE: NEW INTERNA-TIONAL VERSION®, copyright © 1973, 1978, 1984 by the International Bible Society, used by permission of Zondervan Publishing House. All rights reserved. Scripture quotations noted NASB are from the New American Standard Bible, © 1960, 1962, 1963, 1968, 1971, 1972, 1973, 1975, 1977 by The Lockman Foundation. Used by permission.

Printed in the United States of America.

Library of Congress Cataloging-in-Publication Data

Splinter, John P.
   The healing path : a guide for women rebuilding their lives
after sexual abuse / Connie, Marilyn, Brenda, Sharon, Diane,
Caroline with John P. Splinter.
      p.   cm.
   Includes bibliographical references.
   ISBN 0-8407-9251-4 (pbk.)
   1. Adult child sexual abuse victims—Rehabilitation.   2. Abused
women—Mental health.   3. Self-help techniques.   I. Title.
RC569.5.A28S66   1993
616.85'8369—dc20   93-2515
                                                                      CIP

1   2   3   4   5   6   —   98 97 96 95 94 93

To
the many women who have been through
The Healing Touch ministry,
and who have
shared some of their healing journey.

Contents

Acknowledgments   *ix*

Introduction   *1*

1. Beginning the Journey   *7*
2. The Woman   *18*
3. Symptoms of Abuse   *25*
4. Why Me?   *36*
5. Lies!   *47*
6. Looking for Your Mother and Your Child   *63*
7. Profile of an Abuser   *71*
8. The Family System of Abuse   *84*
9. Sexual Abuse and Splitting   *108*
10. Sexual Abuse and Being a Victim   *115*
11. Recognizing Anger   *121*
12. Processing Anger   *131*
13. Victims, Guilt, and Shame   *146*
14. Processing Guilt   *158*
15. No Longer Victims of Fear   *165*
16. Forgiveness: Facing and Leaving Hell   *176*
17. What About God?   *187*
18. Rebuilding a Life, Part I   *201*
19. Rebuilding a Life, Part II   *211*
20. Telling the Tale / Having a Setback   *222*
21. The Last Step   *233*

Notes   *242*

Additional Resources   *244*

Acknowledgments

Although there have been far too many participants in this project to thank them individually by name, I particularly wish to thank all of the women who contributed their experiences and insights to chapter 5, "Lies!"

I would also like to thank Marc Frankel, Ph.D., for his review of several chapters and for his clinical insights provided over the years as this project moved from its earliest phases to the finished reality of a book.

Introduction

This book may be effectively used as a private, home-study guide for individual healing. It can also be used very effectively as a course for sexually abused women. In fact, it was originally written as a course and only later compiled into book format.

IF YOU HAVE BEEN ABUSED

If you wish to use this book as a self-help course in healing after your own abuse, following are some tips.

1. Be sure you have a couple of good friends standing by— women with whom you have regular and open contact and with whom you can share your deepest memories and thoughts. You'll almost certainly need them in the months ahead.

2. Have the name of a good therapist handy in case you need it. It would even be wise to have one preliminary contact with this therapist, just to get to know her. (We recommend Christian female therapists for this task.) Then she'll know more about you if/when you call upon her.

3. Buy a thick, lined notebook, and write your response to every question at the end of the chapters. Also, write your daily progress as you wade into the task of healing after your abuse. Write a lot! We call it journaling. Do it daily. If you aren't comfortable with writing, acquire a tape recorder and audiotapes. The point is to *keep your history* in such a manner that you can readily access and ponder it.

4. Make a contact with the clergy person of your choice, so that if or when the time comes for you to need spiritual input or support, that relationship is also in place.

5. Take one chapter a week as your weekly project. Read the material, journal your responses to the Questions for Reflection, do the Action Items, and reflect upon the spiritual content at the end of each chapter.

6. *If you feel you're getting in over your head, or if you start having a flood of emotions that frightens you, go immediately for help.*

IF YOU WANT TO HELP

The book is laid out in what may be used as weekly segments—one chapter per week. The Questions for Reflection at the end of each chapter may be used to provide a structured way of group interaction with the material in each chapter and will provide a good springboard for therapy.

The most effective use of this material will be within groups led by either trained clinicians or female victims who have grown past most of the pain of their own abuse.

This book is for wounded healers. One doesn't need to be a trained therapist to use the book. If you are an abuse victim yourself, your best tools for helping another female victim are found within your own abuse. If you were abused as a child, then you know more about how it feels to be abused than does any pastor or therapist. You were there—you lived it.

If you are a layperson who has not been a sexual abuse victim, then we would encourage you not to attempt to become involved with sexual abuse victims. Your lack of clinical training and/or personal experience will almost certainly become a detriment to the victim's healing.

FORMING A VICTIMS' RECOVERY GROUP

If you are a victim and don't have access to a group of other sexually abused women but wish you did, following are some ideas as to how to form one.

1. Advertise in a newspaper. Rent a box at the post office to receive answers confidentially, without betraying either yourself or any other woman. Ask for respondents to provide you with their first name (only) and a phone number at which you may reach them (you only). Call the women when they respond. Tell them that you yourself are a victim and have found a book that you'd like to use as a tool for healing. Ask if they would join you in studying the book in a small group.

2. Call your priest or minister and ask if he or she would advertise in the church bulletin. Have all inquiries come to you directly rather than to the minister so that the women may feel protected. Then call the women and tell them you have found a book that you would like to use for everyone's healing. Tell them you'd like to meet in your home for ten to fifteen weeks, studying

one or two chapters per week, and informing them of any other pertinent plans.

3. Call a therapist and ask if she would be willing to begin a small group for sexual abuse victims. Together figure out a strategy for advertising in the community.

4. Contact social agencies such as women's self-help centers, the YWCA, or other groups oriented toward helping people, and ask if they would sponsor a group for women who have been victims. Help them find a person who would act as the facilitator for a group. If none is available, consider volunteering to be that person yourself.

It is not absolutely necessary to be part of a small group in order to process the material in this book. But joining with other victims will give you a far more healing and positive experience.

Guidelines for Small Groups

1. Meet regularly, at the same time and same place each week.

2. Be sure the place is safe and away from prying ears or eyes.

3. Study one chapter each week. Have each woman write her answers to the Questions for Reflection, and insofar as possible have each woman accomplish the Action Items.

4. At each meeting review what each woman has encountered during the week, what she has learned, what struggles she's had, and what goals she is aiming for in the next week.

5. If the group members feel comfortable doing so, begin and end each meeting with a short time of prayer (three to five minutes).

6. Follow agreed-upon ground rules (see the next section).

Ground Rules for Small Groups

If you find or create a small group, having some ground rules will be helpful. Establish them at the first meeting, and thereafter follow them closely. These ground rules are for the protection of everyone in the group.

1. Whatever is shared within the group is to remain there. There are no exceptions to this rule. There will be no dialogue outside the group about matters shared in confidence with the group members.

2. A woman would be asked to leave the group only if the first ground rule were breached.

3. Give advice only when specifically asked for it, and then only sparingly.

4. If advice is given in response to a direct question, limit the advice to your personal experience in the matter. Also, accept the fact that your experience may not be applicable to or correct for another person.

5. Each group member may share her feelings at any time. Yet keep in mind that they are only your own feelings and may not be appreciated by every member of the group.

6. No member may dominate the group by doing most of the talking or by demanding that the group focus mainly upon her issues.

7. If problems of any kind develop with members of the group, these problems will be discussed within the group openly and honestly. But once the group meeting is ended, all discussion of group process and/or group members will cease.

8. Each woman in the group has a personal responsibility to be a positive contributor, leading to the group's success. Each woman is a sister in pain. Decide to build sisterhood. Learn to gain insight and strength from one another. Support one another. Work at issues together. Be on time for meetings. Be sensitive to one another's feelings. Avoid saying or doing anything that would hurt or cause harm to another group member. Be kind, compassionate, and gentle with one another.

Support One Another

If one group member is having a particularly hard struggle, the group should reach out to that person. Call her frequently. Invite her to develop her own safety plan with you. Then, if needed, help her implement that plan. Let her know that you're there for her. Share her load as you are able. Offer encouragement. Pray with her if she wishes to pray. Draw yourselves around her.

The recovery process will no doubt be difficult at times. If this weren't true, each woman in the group would probably have recovered years ago. Expect it to be challenging. Accept that healing won't come easily.

But Keep Appropriate Boundaries

One common mistake many victims make is to attempt to "rescue" another victim from her struggle. You can't rescue another person any more than you can rescue a woman who is giving birth. The struggle is the mother's at that moment. You can't breathe for her; you can't push for her; and you can't scream for her. But you can be there to hold her hand, to speak reassuring words, and to mop her brow. So it is with recovery after abuse. You can encourage and support one another, but the work of healing is each woman's responsibility.

COMMIT YOURSELF TO YOUR OWN HEALING

If you are a victim, the work ahead of you is likely to be extremely challenging. Therefore, do yourself a favor by formally committing yourself to the months or years needed for your own healing. If you are in a small group, you might also pledge to one another that you will stay together until the last chapter is finished.

Realize that there are no quick, magical answers; but *there are real answers*. Commit yourself to a process of healing and growth, starting right now and lasting for your lifetime.

Allow Yourself a "Time-Out" If Needed

Remember, as you progress through this book, you may uncover material that you have repressed for years. If the process of growth gets too scary—if you begin to feel that you may harm yourself—if you feel that you're about to "fall apart"—stop for a while. Give yourself a breather. You may choose to work with a therapist for a few weeks. But don't stop growing or working on your healing, and come back to the material when you're ready. Taking time out is OK, but stopping is not. Stopping means quitting on yourself. Then your perpetrator wins again.

Get Help If You Need Help

If you feel that things are getting out of control, seek help. Don't "white knuckle" it and try to handle it alone. Little children often attempt to keep their lips from quivering and the tears from falling from their eyes, but you are an adult now. It's OK to cry, and it's

OK to seek help. You may need the help of a therapist from time to time. That's OK, and it's normal, considering what you've been through.

Heal by Spiritual Growth

At the end of chapters 3–21, a section entitled For Spiritual Growth contains some biblical references for you to read and reflect upon. You are, among other things, a spiritual being. Those who have helped create this material believe in spiritual as well as emotional healing.

We believe that although it may be profoundly difficult at times to connect with God, especially when we are in the midst of deep pain, He is there, He loves us, and He desires our healing. We encourage you to draw close to God. Trust in the fact that He loves you, even if you don't feel that He could. Reach out to Him as you are able. He has been there for us. God be with you as you grow toward happiness and wholeness.

Chapter 1
Beginning the Journey

"Life is difficult." So begins one of the best books written in recent decades.[1] It's true. Life is difficult—more so for some than for others.

Some persons carry loads that they sometimes feel they cannot share with another human being. This is frequently true of victims of sexual abuse.

There are many things in life that we wish did not happen. Airplanes crash. Children die of cancer. People are mugged. And girls are sexually abused.

Sometimes the abuse is committed by a stranger, but most often it is committed by someone the girl knows and trusts. Frequently, the girl is made to feel that the abuse is her fault, so for the rest of her life she will feel dirty and guilty. She has a "secret" she cannot share. It becomes a load she has to carry, most often alone.

My name is John Splinter and although I wrote this book, I am not the person around whose life the material revolves. In many ways I have merely been the scribe for this book. Although I will tell you more about myself as the book progresses, I can tell you that I am a listener. I am also a writer. But you need to know that the real heart of this material is from a group of courageous women.

Several years ago I received a telephone call from a woman who had just received an obscene phone call. The caller had told her that he had her daughter and would "do things to her" unless she was willing to talk with him.

She talked to him. He asked humiliating questions and she gave humiliating answers. After several minutes of torture she glanced at a clock and realized that her daughter was probably still in school; it was early afternoon. She hung up the phone and called the school, confirmed that her little girl was still in class, put the phone back in its cradle, and came unglued.

She called me, as a friend and also as a minister. I invited her to come to my office, and we began to chat. What unfolded in that conversation was far more significant than the obscene phone call. The caller had hit a profound trigger in her life—one that she had been trying to repress for years: her own childhood sexual abuse.

In a flash, in the midst of the obscene phone call the horrors of her childhood experience had come flooding to conscious memory. She was terrified that her daughter would be forced to undergo a lifetime of agony similar to hers. The experience was overwhelming.

As we sat and talked in my office, memories, feelings, humiliation, bitterness, and guilt all began pouring out of her as if a monstrous dam within her had been breached. Debris was now gushing powerfully, frighteningly, through the breach. After two hours of talking, weeping, and praying, my friend began to settle down enough to return home. But the dam had been broken.

Now repressed thoughts and memories began to fight their way to her consciousness. Anxiety became the password for her every waking moment. No matter how much she tried to force memories and dark thoughts from her mind, they would not go away. In fact, they seemed to be gaining a life of their own.

Anxiety attacks lurked around every corner. She would awaken from frightening dreams in a cold sweat. She was waging a hellish war. We met weekly to talk and pray.

A few months later another woman hesitatingly came to me and hinted that she had been sexually abused as a child. I suggested that we form a small support group. An ongoing group involving several victims soon evolved.

This book is a compilation of material resulting from deeply personal struggles. It does not contain untested, cold, textbook jargon. It is a written reflection of the lives, the pain and the joy, the healing and the wholeness of several very courageous women. It is their story. The book also contains pieces of the stories of scores of women who have used this material since we initially put it into written form.

I've been drawn into this story at least partially because some have seen me as a listener and a healer. I do not consider myself to be a healer, but perhaps my listening is part of others' healing. I have some knowledge of spiritual matters and a small amount of knowledge about the human mind. I have earned master's degrees in both subjects, yet those are only credentials applied when such are needed. Many people in the world have similar credentials, and some of the best healers have neither.

Perhaps my greatest asset is that I have been deeply wounded myself and have attempted to use my own understanding of pain to tune in to other hurting human beings. In a later chapter I'll tell you more about myself and how I came to realize that perhaps I was meant to work on this project.

This book is a tool for healing. If you are a victim, you will find a great amount of support and challenge in this book. You will find permission to grieve and be angry. You will also find ideas for healing, and *healing is challenging*—so challenging that at times it can be difficult without the support of others.

INGREDIENTS FOR HEALING

Your Own Inner Resources

First, *commit yourself to be healed*. Nothing will substitute for your own commitment to yourself and your healing. Second, you will have to *face the past*. What happened to you was bad. It should not have happened—but running away from it won't help you heal. Third, *stay in the present*. After learning to face the past, one of your most important tasks will be learning to live your life in the present. "That was then; this is now" will become your daily password.

This Book

Another important ingredient in your healing will be this well-tested book. It will provide an organized, step-by-step approach to facing many critical issues in your own healing process. It will teach skills and will give tools for healing. Many women have used it for their own healing. But the book will not be sufficient by itself to "heal you." No book can do that.

Individual or Group Therapy

Priscilla, a profoundly damaged woman, went through "The Healing Touch" program twice and is now in personal therapy. She has said that this book was the mechanism by which she opened the door for her own healing. Janet took the book to her therapist, and the two of them used it as a means of working through her abuse issues. Sharon was in a small support group for survivors of incest. Her group built its stages of healing around this book. Alice gave the book to her sister. Both she and her sister were victims, and the two of them worked through it together.

If you are in a therapy group, it should be specifically aimed at recovery after sexual abuse. Milly had been in both individual and group therapy for years, but in all that time she had not brought up the subject of her sexual abuse. She didn't think it was relevant, and the therapist didn't pick up on her victimization. She didn't begin to heal from her abuse until she was able to bring her issues into the open within a survivor's group.

Other Books

There are many excellent self-help books on the market. At the end of the book will be a list of additional resources to provide more information on the various tasks of healing. But I'll repeat that reading won't be enough. You're going to need personal support as you learn to act upon what you read.

Sharing Your Journey with Other Women

Sexual abuse is usually a closely guarded secret. As you read through this book, you'll be challenged to bring your secret into the light of day and to find other women with whom you can share your story. Although you may find that process difficult, you will also find it healing.

Consider seeking out one or two "sisters" with whom you may share your story and who will walk with you as you progress through this book. As we are wounded relationally, so we are healed relationally. We heal best when connected to others who love us.

One note of caution: each woman's journey will be unique. Don't compare your progress with anyone else. Don't feel that if you are not whizzing along comfortably toward total wholeness within a month, you're a failure. Healing from sexual abuse takes time. Your own healing might take longer than you had initially envisioned, and it will take lots of challenging work on your part.

Don't be afraid of it. You are worth the effort. In fact, you might make a little handwritten sign and put in on your refrigerator: _"I am worth the effort!"_

HOW TO BEST USE THIS BOOK

Try reading one chapter each week. If you have a couple of "sisters" with whom you can share your insights and growth, do so on a weekly basis. However, whether or not you have anyone with whom you can share, do your daily journaling. _At the very least, write in a notebook your own answers to the questions at the end of each chapter._ Be thorough. Answer each question. Your writing will become your own path of healing, to read and reread in the months ahead.

Sharing is frightening but important. It is risky to share, and you will want to be selective, sharing primarily with your two chosen friends at first. Yet one of the women in our own support group is now standing before audiences and saying, "When I was a child I was sexually abused. I want to tell you about this because I suspect there are some women in this audience who have been abused, and I want you to know there is hope." Sharing is an important key to growth and healing.

If your sexual abuse occurred when you were an adult, you may still find this book helpful. Adult rape victims have used this book and have found it supportive and helpful.

As you read this book you will be challenged to move toward the goal of openly sharing and discussing your own story, at your own speed, in your own time, in your own way. If your abuse occurred when you were a child, then it is possible that you are facing the most difficult task in your life. It is probable that your sense of self-esteem is profoundly damaged. It is probable that you carry many patterns of victim-like relationships that began in your childhood.

As a victim you almost undoubtedly carry feelings of guilt, anger, helplessness, hopelessness, bitterness, a sense of being stained, and possibly strong feelings that "you must keep this a secret."

THERE IS HOPE FOR YOU

The women who have provided the basis for this book can tell you that *there is hope. There is healing.* It may take some time, perhaps even some years. There may be some difficult battles in the months ahead. But there is hope, and you are not alone. It is possible to have a very happy, healthy, and even *normal* life after being sexually abused.

As you progress through this book, you will find that there are three basic sources of healing. They will come to you in the form of your relationships among:

1. Yourself and yourself (self-acceptance, self-forgiveness, self-nurturing);

2. Yourself and God (spiritual growth, trust, and reaching out for God);

3. Yourself and other women (social growth).

Obviously, for many the most difficult challenge will be the healing of relationships between yourself and men. For now we'll identify your relationships with men as an eventual objective of healing, but not a source of it.

Note that the factor of your relationships with women is listed as the third source of healing, not the first. Many victims have verbalized enormous issues to be overcome in their relationships with their mothers. These issues are frequently translated into relational problems with other women in general. Yet trusting, caring, and nurturing relationships with other women will be a source of healing for you as you progress, if you allow them to do so.

As you progress through this book you will be challenged to face some powerful and painful matters in your life. You will not be forced to face them, but you will be led to them. You may choose to ignore them. The only person to whom you must answer is yourself.

You have probably spent a great deal of energy avoiding many issues to be recalled in the chapters ahead. You may make some self-discoveries that will feel overwhelming.

One victim has said that beginning the process of her own healing was somewhat like opening Pandora's box. Once the lid was opened and the ingredients were out, it was impossible to put the lid back on and stop the process.

IT'S OK TO SEEK HELP

If, through this process, you begin to fear loss of control, seek professional help. It's OK to ask for help.

Following are some things that are normal and OK as you wade into this material:

- It's OK to be afraid and to experience deep anger.
- It can be normal to experience anxiety attacks.
- It can be normal to experience depression.
- It can be normal to have nightmares.
- It's OK to cry or to scream.
- It's OK to talk openly about what you're experiencing or what you experienced in the past.

Sexual abuse is profound. It attacks the core of who you are. It takes hold of its victims' self-esteem and twists and rips it. It usually leaves its victims feeling shredded, wilted, stained, and ugly. It is so wretched that most victims work very hard at keeping it locked away tightly in a remote "closet of the mind." Many victims assume, at least for a few years, that they have it mastered, that it's not a part of their lives, that it doesn't affect them—that it's something that happened a long time ago but doesn't matter now.

However, within that remote closet are switches and levers that the "dragon" of abuse can manipulate. As one matures, she begins to recognize that many "symptoms" or quirks of attitude, behavior, or perception are coming from the dragon's use of his closet technology.

As you begin to pry open the doors of the closet, you may reexperience many feelings from the time of your abuse. Memories are often carried forward in time by feelings. As you process being fondled or raped as a child, you may actually experience again some of the feelings of fear, helplessness, and (if you're lucky) rage that you quickly repressed as a child.

Those feelings build and shape the dragon in your closet. If you attempt to convince yourself that he is not there or is not real, he'll just stay in the closet and work his covert manipulations upon your life and relationships.

If you open the door and turn the light on, he might come tumbling out and make you feel terrified or as if you're going crazy. The thing to remember in this process is that whether or not you admit that there's a dragon in your closet, he's there.

The way to beat him is to open the door, let him pour out his scourge of horrors, and finally beat him back with your newly discovered self-esteem.

It takes energy to keep closets locked up. It takes energy to hide dragons. It takes energy to keep secrets. While those secrets may be horrible and frightening, they are limited in their power. At this stage in your life, the most they can do is to frighten you.

The only real weapons your secrets have are the feelings that you couldn't allow yourself to experience or express when you were being abused. You might find those feelings to be as strong now as they were when you were a child. That too is normal. This book will help you learn how to diminish those feelings.

This resource will help you learn the process of opening the closet doors, letting the dragon vent his wrath, then sweeping him out of the house, turning on the lights, and airing out the whole house. This book is about having no more secrets, no more energy given to hiding things, no more time wasted with feelings of dirtiness, guilt, and the like.

As you read and do your daily journaling you will be faced with a constant "growing edge," a constant choice: to grow or to retreat. Healing from sexual abuse can be compared to healing from a surgically removed ruptured appendix. Surgery is painful; but as the surgeon removes the poisonous item from the body, the opportunity for new wholeness is born.

Nobody can take healing steps for you. You must learn to walk as a whole adult. You may feel unbelievably alone at times. Remember, you are not alone. God is with you. Furthermore, you share in a painful secret that affects the lives of 20 to 33 percent of all women. You may not know who they are, but you have thousands of sisters.

Remember too, whether you can see it now or not, *there is light at the end of the tunnel. There is healing. There is hope. There is wholeness*. Even after profound abuse.

Each of the women whose lives provided the basis for this book had a major setback during the time we met. Each woman faced some experience or insight that caused her to temporarily regress in her growth. There will be times when you feel as if you're going backward rather than forward. That's normal too. If you're an incest victim, consider family reunions to be major setback opportunities.

WORK THROUGH YOUR FEELINGS

It can be normal to feel crazy at times of deep stress in our lives. However, don't consider yourself to *be* crazy, even if you *feel* crazy. Rather than applying the word *crazy* to yourself, choose words such as *hurting, frightened, confused, disoriented,* or *angry*.

As you process your own memories and feelings, keep reminding yourself that *you are a survivor*. You were abused, and you survived it. You have enormous inner reserves, which have given you the strength to make it thus far in your life. Right? You're not crazy. You're a survivor. You have developed coping skills that have helped you survive.

Your abuse experiences may have led you to handle some of your relationships in ways that don't work very well. That too is normal. If you begin to recognize some rather dysfunctional components of personality or relationship operating in yourself, relax. You deserve the luxury of a few kooky things, given what you've been through.

As you heal and grow, you may decide to change a few things in yourself in order to more fully enjoy yourself or your relationships. Give yourself permission to do so in your own way, at your own speed.

Some victims find themselves terrified of men. Others are repulsed by men. Some become promiscuous with men. All of these behaviors, plus any others you may name, are rational when put into the framework and experience of the individual victim. They represent what works for each victim. As you progress through this book you will discover keys to changing your attitudes, perceptions, and behavior in regard to men. If you choose to change in this way, that's fine. If not, that's fine too.

What happened to you was wrong. It should not have happened. You are not at fault. You don't have to live with the negative legacy of the abuse. You can heal. There is hope. Now is the time to begin opening the closet and airing out the whole house. Now is the time for you to begin using your energy, all of it, for tasks other than keeping secrets and fighting hidden dragons.

In subsequent chapters you will discover various stages of healing. You will read several short instances of many women's stories. More important for you to know than each woman's specific story is the process, the stages of healing and growth. With one exception that process will be the focus of this book. The exception is found in the next chapter, "The Woman." This chapter is provided so that you may understand that even within the most wretched abuse, there is hope.

It is our prayer that you will emerge from the tangled and dark woods of abuse into the light of freedom, happiness, freshness, health, self-respect, and peace, and that you will never again live as a victim. God be with you.

QUESTIONS FOR REFLECTION

If you're not in a small group, acquire a notebook and write at least one paragraph in answer to each of the "Questions for Reflection" at the end of each chapter. Avoid the temptation to just review each question, thinking that you have the answer to each one in your head. Take some time. Invest in yourself. Write your answers in some depth.

1. Reflect upon whether you feel that spiritual healing of any kind is significant as you attempt to heal after having been a victim. If so, what does spiritual healing mean to you?

2. Reflect upon what has brought you to this moment in your life. Why are you seeking healing at this moment, as compared with any previous time in your life?

3. Reflect upon your own determination to heal. How deep is your commitment to yourself? How "steeled" are you for what is ahead of you?

4. Reflect upon what is most frightening about healing. As you anticipate what may lie ahead, what is the most scary aspect? Why?

5. If you had a magic wand and could wave it to create a whole new you, what would she look, act, think, and feel like? (Have some fun writing about this.)

≡ ACTION ITEMS ≡

1. Buy a large notebook, and begin your writing, called "journaling," today. Write in your notebook every day, and date each entry. Record your thoughts, feelings, experiences, insights, and answers to questions from this book. By the time you're finished with this book you may have filled more than one such notebook. In this way you'll have a written record of your journey.

2. Make a pledge to yourself to do one thing every day to keep yourself growing and going forward. Do this until you are completely satisfied that you have overcome the effects of your abuse. Your reward will be a happy and peaceful life and self-esteem that is whole.

Chapter 2
The Woman

What you are about to read may shock you.

This book is an attempt to deal straightforwardly with what may be one of the last closet issues of our culture. It's an ugly issue, wrapped in shame, decorated with vile memories, and stamped with pain. This issue is sexual violation of children.

The story in this chapter is real. It's a composite story, blended together from the lives of more than one victim. This blending was done in order to protect the identities of the victims. All of the events really happened.

This is a brutal story, one that may offend your sensibilities. Actually, if it doesn't offend you, if you can read it without feeling sad and angry, something's wrong. It's a shocking and deeply moving story. But it is not included for shock value. In fact, some of the most gruesome details have been deleted. It is included in this book in order to open the door to a candid discussion of sexual abuse.

The story you are about to read is that of a victim. It's a story not only of sexual abuse, but also of violence. If you are a victim, your abuse may not have been this wretched. Yet you are a victim. Your abuse may not have been of this type. Still, you are a victim. Don't think for a moment, even if your abuse was not this bad, that you're not a victim or that your need for healing is not significant or considerable.

Many bits and pieces of this story will be discussed in subsequent chapters. As you read the story, note the sick family system of abuse. Note the isolation of the victim. Note her desperate feelings. Note the relationship between the victim and her mother. Note the victim's helplessness. Note some of the survival techniques she discovers. Note her denial of self-value, her desire for death. Note who reaches out to help her. And now, meet the victim.

She was a pretty little girl, or so she has been told by her aunt. Her childhood pictures show what some would call "a pretty little girl." But she feels so distant, so removed from those pictures—almost as if that little girl were someone else.

She remembers wearing blue jeans and playing hard, getting sweaty. She remembers wearing a pretty dress once in a while and feeling very delicate.

She remembers her mother as busy—always busy. Too much to do and too little time to get it all done. Mom was crabby a lot. Sick a lot too. Gone a lot too, now that she thinks of it. Not exactly what a little girl would have chosen in a mother, but she was Mom.

She remembers the first time it happened. She was taking a bath. Suddenly Daddy was in the bathroom, "helping her wash." It didn't feel right. She was too old for anyone to be helping her bathe. She saw a look in Daddy's eyes, too. It was a scary look. He was breathing as if he'd been out jogging.

She didn't say anything about it to anyone. She was confused and humiliated that Daddy touched her there. A few months passed. Then one day when Mom was gone (she can't remember where), Daddy came into her room and told her that the time had come for him to "help her understand a few things about being a big girl." It was to be a sort of game, Daddy said, and it was to be their secret—only their secret. Mom wasn't to be told, even though Daddy said that it was OK with Mom.

The game began by undressing. She'd never felt so embarrassed and humiliated in all her life. She was naked in front of her father, and he was naked in front of her. Then he began touching her again, this time with more passion. Soon his hand was rubbing her and his fingers.... Oh, God! *she silently screamed.* What's going on! This is frightening me! I don't like this!

After that it was just a matter of time until Daddy "helped her" understand what intercourse was all about. Usually it happened while Mom was gone, but as time progressed it even happened when Mom was home. Then came other things, more of the many things she hates to remember. She remembers gagging and wishing she could die.

One time when Daddy was abusing her he ridiculed her because she was so flat chested. She was only a little girl, perhaps ten years old at the time, but of course it didn't matter. Dad was disappointed with her, as usual. He had started calling her horrible names too.

As she began to develop a figure, the abuse got worse. Once she ran outside and hid, trying to refuse him. That was the time Daddy got a gun and threatened to kill her baby sister. Mom pleaded with her "not to do such a terrible thing," so she gave up and went back into the trap.

From time to time she fantasized about killing herself. How would she do it? Would she leave a note? Would she send a letter to the police, to her teachers at school, to a neighbor, and then die? No. She remembers thinking that if she did, Daddy would go to jail and the family would be destroyed. Or even worse, nothing would happen.

The most humiliating event in her life occurred one evening when her uncle came to visit. He'd been drinking, as usual. She was about thirteen years old now and had developed into a mature young lady. Daddy and Uncle drank some more. Then Daddy called her into the bedroom where he and Uncle were standing, leering at her with reddened, drunken eyes.

"Show him," Daddy said.

"What?" she said in confusion.

"Show him what you've got!"

There was nowhere to run, and soon she was standing in front of two drunken men, naked from the waist up. Then they took turns using her and laughing.

By this time she had found that she could make her mind go some-

where else. She was learning that she could even keep from "feeling" certain parts of her body when bad things were happening to her.

Things got worse. The next morning when she came into the kitchen, her eyes swollen from a sleepless night of crying, Mom said, "So what's wrong with you?" When she made a careful attempt at telling what had happened to her, Mom called Daddy into the kitchen. They made her undress so they could perform a vaginal exam, to "see if she was still a virgin."

That evening was the first time she tried to kill herself. She remembers that when she awoke in the hospital, she was wildly, desperately angry with God for not allowing her the grace to just die.

As terrible as things had become, they now became even more confusing. Mom began to pour out anger upon her and became violent toward her. Sometimes Mom intentionally burned her by rubbing lit cigarette butts on her body. Once Mom even took a pair of pliers and ripped part of her face off.

She remembers thinking, If I don't get out of here, eventually they'll kill me—if I don't kill myself first. *With no money, no job, and no place to go, she took a couple of blankets and left home. That night she slept in some bushes a few blocks from home.*

A few days later she met Richard. He came from a bad home too; both of his parents were alcoholics and beat him. He offered her a place to stay for the night, and she took it. On the second night he told her that he wanted to make love with her. Since her father had told her many times that sex was all she was good for, she shrugged. Why not. *It wasn't enjoyable. Parts of her body were numb, and her mind was a million miles away. Yet at the same time she vividly remembered similar experiences with Daddy, Uncle, and her brothers.*

She moved to another town. She tried going to church once, but she felt so dirty she couldn't stand it. She left partway through the second hymn. She knew that God hated her. Mom had told her that God hated people who were sexually active, and Mom was a deeply religious person. Well, for that matter, so was Daddy. In fact, he was a deacon and sang in the choir. So much for God.

Pregnancy and abortion went hand in hand. Her reputation began to spread. People knew about her. She was "one of those." She always wondered why so many "good" men seemed to want her sexually, in spite of her reputation. She became more and more numb inside.

Oddly, it was another woman who finally reached out to her. She doesn't remember how they met, but Sally had been a victim too. They wound up sitting in some restaurant, talking.

Sally was saying that there was hope, that there could be wholeness again. She was saying that God loved her. Yeah, God, she thought, the one that let all this happen to me. She heard Sally say, "I care about you, and I want to help you. You are a precious person. Please let me be your friend."

She remembers crying—just a tear or two at first. But when Sally touched her arm she couldn't hold her feelings back any longer. A torrent of tears burst out, as if they'd been waiting for years for just this moment. She wept unashamedly. For some reason it felt all right to cry. She was safe. It felt so good to cry again. She remembers laying her head on Sally's shoulder and bawling like a baby.

That night in her apartment, in the dark, she lay on her bed staring at the ceiling. She said, "God, are You there? Do You know me? Do You care about what's happened to me? I can't go on living like this. I need Your help. Please help me. Either help me or let me die."

It took many years to heal completely. In fact, she says she's still healing. But once the healing started, she never wanted to go back. She remembers feeling pure, whole, and clean for the first time in her life.

Yesterday she told her story to a group of women. All of them were sexual abuse victims. Many of them cried as she told her story. She knew they were crying from their own pain. Most of them said they didn't believe they could ever feel what she described—clean, pure, whole. But she knows it's true.

The last thing she said to them was, "Let me introduce you to my very best friend in the world. He is the One who put His hand on my life instead of my body, showed me what real love was all about, wiped the slate clean again, and gave me back my life in a fresh new way."

MEET ANOTHER WOMAN—
ANOTHER VICTIM

Then one of the Pharisees asked Jesus to a meal with him. When Jesus came into the house, he took his place at the table and a woman, known in the town as a bad woman, found out that Jesus was there and brought an alabaster flask of perfume and stood behind him crying, letting her tears fall on his feet and then drying them with her hair. Then she kissed them and anointed them with the perfume. When the Pharisee who had invited him saw this, he said to himself, "If this man were really a prophet, he would know who this woman is and what sort of person is touching him. He would have realized that she is a bad woman."

Then Jesus spoke to him.

"Simon, there is something I want to say to you."

"Very well, master," he returned, "say it."

"Once upon a time, there were two men in debt to the same moneylender. One owed him fifty dollars and the other five. And since they were unable to pay, he generously canceled both of their debts. Now, which one of them do you suppose will love him more?"

"Well," returned Simon, "I suppose it will be the one who has been more generously treated."

"Exactly," replied Jesus, and then turning to the woman, he said to Simon:

"You can see this woman? I came into your house but you provided no water to wash my feet. But she has washed my feet with her tears and dried them with her hair. There was no warmth in your greeting, but she, from the moment I came in, has not stopped covering my feet with kisses. You gave me no oil for my head, but she has put perfume on my feet. That is why I tell you, Simon, that her sins, many as they are, are forgiven; for she has shown me so much love. But the man who has little to be forgiven only has a little love to give."

Then he said to her,

"Your sins are forgiven."

And the men at the table with him began to say to themselves, "And who is this man, who even forgives sins?"

But Jesus said to the woman:

"It is your faith that has saved you. Go in peace" (Luke 7:36–50 PHILLIPS).

Among victims there is a tendency to downplay their abuse. You may read this story and say, "Well, my situation certainly wasn't as bad as that!" If you are a victim and can say that, fine. But even if your story is not as emotionally, physically, or spiritually painful as this one, you are still a victim. Don't measure your abuse against what happened in this story. Measure it only against your reaction to it, your feelings, your memories, your relationships, and your self-esteem.

Measure your being a victim against your ability to trust people. Measure it against your ability to have good, healthy, open, fun, even spontaneous relationships with both men and women. Measure your victimization against the impact it has had upon one person: you.

It's OK to hurt if the hurting has a purpose, a direction, and an end. Continue to read to be healed yourself. And if you start hurting, remember the Healer, the One whom Sally knew. Meet the victim's "very best friend in the world," the One who had touched her life rather than her body and, in that touch, gave her back her life.

Chapter 3
Symptoms of Abuse

Sexual abuse is a widely varied subject and takes many forms. Following are a few variations. This is not an exhaustive list—just a sampling. If you have been subjected to any of these, consider yourself to be a victim of sexual abuse.

- Touched in sexual areas (fondled, grabbed, or other)
- Raped
- Made to touch another person sexually
- Made to pose for sexual photographs or movies
- Made to watch movies in which sex was the predominant theme
- Talked to in sexual ways that made you feel dirty
- Encouraged or manipulated into sexual acts with which you were not comfortable

- Bathed in a manner that felt invasive
- Made to participate in prostitution or pornography
- Subjected to humiliating conversation that revolved around your body or your sexuality
- Told you were not much good for anything but sex
- Offered money for any sexually related act or conversation

Sexual abuse is coming "out of the closet." Studies vary, but they usually indicate that between 20 percent and 33 percent of all girls will be sexually abused before their eighteenth birthday. This means that everyone probably knows someone who has been abused. It is usually a closely guarded, painfully embarrassing secret.

Devalued self-esteem is the currency of sexual abuse. Victims frequently feel dirty, guilty, and ashamed of their involvement, even though they had little or no choice in the matter. If the abuse was not overtly forced but covertly accomplished through manipulation and deceit, the victim often feels especially dirty. She may think, *I had a choice, and still I went to him. I must be really sick.* Many victims somehow believe that they brought upon themselves the horrors of their abuse. The bottom line is that sexual abuse tramples a victim's self-esteem.

Sexual abuse leaves emotional scars. Many victims report an internal, anguished cry. Victims often find themselves helpless before the feelings that arise from abusive memories. Even taking a big risk and talking about the abuse doesn't seem to get them past the feelings and memories. In fact, many victims find that at the beginning of the healing process, talking about their abuse seems to make the memories and feelings worse.

So they try to forget again. When the feelings and memories resurface, many women simply change their conscious thoughts and refuse to dwell upon the memories any longer. This is called *suppression.* "I just won't think about it, and then it'll go away."

But it doesn't go away. Instead, those memories often become like a dead fish in a cardboard box—the smell just seems to grow worse. Sometimes the memories and feelings are so painful that the victim "forgets" them. This is called *repression* and happens when the conscious mind simply is unable to recall the pain. Phew! It's gone!

But not really. It's still there, but now there's a wall between the victim and the smelly cardboard box. She can't see the box any longer; but it still stinks. That wall is called *the repressive barrier*—a term used to describe things that lie outside of conscious recall.

The memories remain in the mind, and they still exert influence over victims' attitudes, perceptions, and behavior. They still pull strings from somewhere back in their dark closets. They can often be brought back to conscious recall through such tools as hypnosis, psychotherapy, and an occasional nightmare or dream. Frequently they seem to "leak" out through feelings. Feelings can result in emotional impulses—sometimes so strong that one feels overwhelmed by them—irrational fears, or drives.

Imagine a situation for a moment. You're sitting in a dentist's chair. You have an incredible, pounding toothache. Feel the pain. It's awful. Your mandibular joint—indeed, your whole jaw—is swollen. You've lost weight because you can't chew food without severe pain. You can't sleep at night. Now the dentist tells you that you have a severely abscessed tooth. He must perform oral surgery, and after the surgery you may have even more pain until the stitches and medication begin to effect healing. He says that in a matter of time the pain will subside and you'll be able to resume normal life.

That's not a bad analogy of healing from deep struggles such as sexual abuse. In fact, healing a toothache is much easier to accomplish than healing a heartache. The symptoms are more socially acceptable. They don't imply anything about one's character. They don't represent an embarrassing history.

Let's use another analogy. Imagine a tall glass of milk. The glass was clean when the milk was poured in. Now imagine the milk being poured out. What's left is a filmy residue. Think of the milk as representing the experiences of our lives. The filmy residue is the feelings and memories that are left after our experiences have passed. This residue can last a lifetime, especially if we work diligently at suppressing or repressing our memories and feelings. Like the abscessed tooth, the symptoms will probably remain until the cause of the pain is treated.

Many victims deny that what happened to them long ago has any bearing upon their present lives. "Heck, that was something that happened to me when I was just a kid. It doesn't mean anything to me now. I'm a grown woman, for crying out loud!" Yet victims frequently find that symptoms emerge from some murky depth.

Even when repressed or suppressed, symptoms remain and take control, refusing to allow rational thinking.

SYMPTOMS OF VICTIMIZATION

What are some of these symptoms? Following is a short list.

1. Feeling the need for perfectionism in all aspects of life: relationships, vocation, daily living.

2. Having a sense of overwhelming guilt, a feeling of always being wrong—especially in relationships.

3. Feeling a constant need to make up for being a bad girl, therefore driving oneself to achieve in most areas of life.

4. Having low self-esteem.

5. Feeling dirty, bad, ashamed, guilty.

6. Feeling that if people really knew you they would reject you because of what happened to you.

7. Feeling self-hatred, even to the point of wishing self-mutilation or self-destruction.

8. Feeling like damaged goods, not worthy of others' love; if married, feeling especially unworthy of a spouse's love.

9. Having difficulty in accepting genuine acceptance, love, and caring from nearly everyone.

10. Having difficulty in trusting one's own thought processes and feelings; feeling that the other person must be right most of the time.

11. Feeling confused or disoriented much of the time.

12. Feeling unable to deal with strong feelings, especially anger.

13. Repeatedly struggling with depression, nightmares, anxiety attacks, or fears of going crazy.

14. Fearing when people get too emotionally close to you.

15. Having difficulty in making commitments to others.

16. Becoming a "problem solver" or a "nurturing mother type" for many people.

17. Frequently clinging to people who seem to need you, even when they make you angry.

18. Frequently "testing" people who say they love you, just to see if they really do.

19. Having difficulty in trusting people.

20. Struggling with compulsive behavior patterns, including

overeating or undereating, being a "neatnik," doing seemingly ritualistic things again and again, and so on.

21. Living with an overwhelming need to please, coupled with a self-image dependent upon how well you please others.

22. Living with a need to "perform"—to do whatever others may ask of you, since you see your needs as secondary to the needs of others.

23. Avoiding sexual encounters.

24. Feeling that your value is primarily in your sexuality (the opposite of symptom 23).

25. Using sex to meet needs that are not sexual—for example, to feel loved, to be held, to feel that you're important.

26. Feeling that sex is distasteful or disgusting.

27. Having flashbacks.

28. Experiencing anger, sometimes inappropriate, just waiting for an opportunity to boil over.

29. Fearing that you may lose control of your emotions.

30. Desperately fearing that your children may end up experiencing what you did; constant hovering over them or at least feeling anxiety about them, particularly as they reach the age at which you were abused.

31. Finding yourself abusing your own children and not understanding why.

32. Having difficulty in feeling emotionally close to your children—or, conversely, being overinvolved with or overprotective of them.

33. When with your childhood family, feeling out of control, frightened, unimportant, angry, or depressed.

34. Feeling a need to protect your family from the knowledge of what happened to you.

35. Feeling a real dislike of your own body; trying to deny certain aspects of the way your body looks.

36. Having numbness in certain parts of your body from time to time (especially areas that are used sexually).

37. Dealing with physical illnesses that you suspect may in some way be associated with your abuse.

38. Wishing to hurt your body sometimes, perhaps to cut off certain parts of your body.

39. Having recurring thoughts such as: Something's wrong

with me. I was seductive—I wanted the abuse. I am dirty and stained forever. I am alone, and I exist to be taken advantage of. I am only good for sex. I deserved to be abused. I deserve only bad things.

40. Seeking peace and safety at any price.

41. Having a general feeling of hopelessness, both about yourself and life in general.

42. Experiencing a deep and irrational hatred for some person who has not necessarily abused you, but could have.

43. Feeling that you should be able to grow up and move beyond all these intrusive thoughts about your abuse—but you can't seem to do it.

44. Feeling envy of other women who have "normal" lives.

45. Fearing that if you let go of your anger, you might kill someone, kill yourself, never be able to regain control, or go crazy.

To understand the healing process, go back in your mind to the dentist's chair. Remember the abscessed tooth? In order for the dentist to fix it, he may have to do some cutting and drilling, and there may be some blood at first. Yet there is healing at the end of pain. So as you progress through the material in this book, ask yourself, "How long do I want to live with the abscess?"

You're beginning a journey. It's your own personal journey toward a healthy, happy future. The route to healing may involve peeling away some protective layers that you have built into your life—a challenging and frightening process. You may feel vulnerable for a while. You may encounter feelings of anger, guilt, shame, sadness, and fear that you thought you'd safely tucked away or forgotten.

As you read, keep remembering that this book was created by women who have been victims of sexual abuse. They have felt what you feel. They aren't experts who studied child abuse in textbooks and then created a lot of easy answers. They were touched. They were forced. They were manipulated. They have lived for years with the humiliation of having been objects. They know what it's like to feel guilty and dirty. They had the same secrets you do.

Layer by layer, their protective tissues were peeled away and opened to the light. They had to learn to trust another person. So do you. They had to share their secrets. So do you. From risking enough to tell their stories, they learned that they could be loved in spite of their experiences. At first each woman was completely convinced that she was unlovable. Not one felt she had any hope of real recovery. If you feel that way, then you are not alone.

As the women went through months of sharing together, they found spiritual insights. They became better acquainted with their need for God and discovered that by drawing closer to Him, their healing process was accelerated and strengthened. They found that through prayer, they were given strength to push through barriers that seemed insurmountable.

The overriding message of this book is that there is hope. It is possible to feel clean again. It is possible to be normal. It is possible to be married, to be in love, and to enjoy a happy and healthy sex life. It is possible to be held by a man without fearing abuse or having flashbacks. It is possible to find genuine love and caring in the world. You are not forever doomed to a life of hiding, secrets, shame, and compensating for your experiences.

There is fresh air, freedom, and purity awaiting you. Your symptoms, whatever they are, make sense. You are not crazy. Considering your experiences, perhaps it's normal for you to feel crazy. Therefore, as you begin to look at your life, keep telling yourself, *My symptoms make sense. They serve a purpose. I'm not crazy. Everything I do or think or feel is OK. I'm a survivor. I'm good at it!*

POSTTRAUMATIC STRESS DISORDER

After each war there are soldiers who become mentally incapable of living a normal life, at least for a while. They have been too close to death. They have seen too many body parts blown away. They have another set of symptoms, called posttraumatic stress disorder, or PTSD.

Sometimes these men just go blank. They stare at a wall for hours. Sometimes they are reduced to whimpering and can't remember much of anything. Sometimes they can remember everything except the hottest part of the battle. The effects vary. The purpose of PTSD is to protect the fragile, terrorized ego from further trauma.

Sexual abuse victims frequently develop self-defense personality traits similar to those of soldiers struggling with PTSD. PTSD is a relatively common response to immense stress. It may come about as a result of any catastrophic event outside the range of normal human experience: rape, an attempt on one's life, a serious car crash, fire, earthquake, tornado, bombing, torture, extreme physical violence, sexual abuse, and others. These experiences leave people feeling terrified, helpless, and (often) under some physical duress.

PTSD is significant enough that it is now listed in the American Psychiatric Association's official diagnostic manual. The February 1991 *Harvard Mental Health Letter* addressed the subject.

> In the posttraumatic reaction, which may begin days, weeks, months, or even years later, three types of symptoms emerge. *FIRST,* victims involuntarily reexperience the traumatic event in the form of intrusive memories, nightmares, and flashbacks during which they feel or even act as though the event were recurring.
>
> (*SECOND*) Alternating with these reminders of the experience is an opposing group of symptoms—avoidance of feelings, thoughts, and situations reminiscent of the trauma, numbing of normal emotional responses, or both. In the effort to avoid thinking about the experience, victims may even completely forget important aspects of it. More generally, they often succumb to a kind of emotional anesthesia.
>
> Yet they are hypersensitive rather than insensitive to the feelings that constitute a (*THIRD*) group of symptoms. They are edgy, irritable, nervously watchful, and easily startled. They sleep poorly and find it difficult to concentrate. Some are tense with barely stifled rage and occasionally lose control in violent outbursts.[1]

Another issue of the *Harvard Mental Health Letter* suggested that treatment for the PTSD victim should provide "a way for the patient to feel safe in confronting the traumatic event and linking it emotionally as well as intellectually to the symptoms. Patients must learn now to think about the trauma without intrusive reliving, and exercise self-control without avoidance and emotional numbing."[2]

Sexual abuse often causes great trauma to its victims. Sometimes the experience is not processed by the mind until years after the event. To recognize its impact upon her, sometimes a woman must look at symptoms that don't make sense until interpreted *through the lens of sexual abuse.*

In order to heal, a woman must return to "the scene of the accident." Doing so will probably stir up some old feelings that she would rather ignore. Perhaps she thought the old feelings were gone.

One of the creators of this book said that she had been in individual and group therapy for some time and had discussed all sorts of life events, but had never mentioned that when she was young her brothers had raped her. She didn't think this information had much to do with any of her present-day problems.

Your sexual abuse may be the core issue around which many personality and relationship difficulties have been woven throughout your life. Listen to your symptoms. They are telling you something.

QUESTIONS FOR REFLECTION

1. Reread the list of symptoms and consider which ones you have noticed in your life, especially within the last six months. Why do you think they may be present? What purpose might they serve? Do they protect you in any way? If so, how? Do they remind you of negative feelings or thoughts? If so, which ones?

2. Reflect upon your ability to allow yourself to get emotionally close to people. Do you have a problem with close relationships? In what way might this be associated with your abuse?

3. Recall some strong feelings you have had within the past six months. In what way do you suspect these feelings might be associated with your abuse? Are there any logical connections?

4. Consider this question: If within the next year you were going to share your story (or as much of it as you can remember), with whom would you share it, and how would you go about sharing it?

5. What was the most interesting discovery you made in this chapter? Why is that discovery so significant to you?

6. As you read the symptoms of posttraumatic stress disorder, did you recognize any of the traits as yours? If so, that's OK. It's normal. Your abuse may have been far more traumatic than you have realized.

≡ *ACTION ITEMS* ≡

Copy the following in your notebook, in your own handwriting.

Today I am beginning to open the doors.
It may be a long time before I can pry some of them open.
I have hidden many memories behind them.
I may become frightened as I begin opening these doors.
I may become very angry as I open them.
I may weep and experience desperate sadness.
I may experience a sense of being more alone than I have ever
    dared to imagine.
But today I am beginning to open doors.

Today I have charted my course.
I am not going to turn back now.
I am committed to my tomorrows, to new freedom, to feeling
    pure again, and to healthy relationships.
I am committed to myself.
I am worthy of my commitment.

I have been abused.
Today I will begin sharing my story, as I am able.
I will not keep it a secret any longer.
I don't want to carry this burden one more day of my life.
I want to feel clean and pure again.
I want to look people in the eyes and smile warmly, openly. I
    want to know that they love me.

Today I am willing to let God help me.
I will not ask Him to do for me that which I am
    not willing to do for myself.
Yet I know there is healing that only He can
    accomplish within me—healing that I cannot
    do alone.

Today I am going to begin to let other women help me too.
They don't have all the answers, but they can help me learn to
    trust again.

Today I am beginning to open the doors.

I want the wholeness of sunlight and happiness in my life.

Although I can't change the past, I can begin to shape my todays and my tomorrows.

Today I begin. This is my journey toward wholeness. I will not turn back.

FOR SPIRITUAL GROWTH

1. Proverbs 15:13 says, "A joyful heart makes a cheerful face, /But when the heart is sad, the spirit is broken" (NASB). What do you think your heart, your spirit, and your face are communicating to those who know you?

2. Proverbs 16:3 says, "Commit your works to the LORD" (NKJV). How may this concept be applied to your own process of healing? Is God really interested in your healing? Are you? Are you willing to commit your healing to the hands of God?

Chapter 4
Why Me?

A common question victims ask is, "Why me? How did he select me as his victim? What vulnerability did I communicate to him? Did I appear to want his attention? Was I unknowingly seductive?"

It is important to begin with one fact: *Nobody has the right to sexually abuse a child.* It doesn't matter how a child's actions are perceived by an adult. *Nobody* has the right to sexually molest a child, even if the perpetrator is able to manipulate the child into giving full consent. It is wrong and *criminal* for an adult to do so.

But the question remains: How did your perpetrator select you? Was it just a random act, or was some planning involved? It is likely that your abuser gave a great deal of thought to his actions. He probably set up the circumstances through which he could abuse you. He may have somehow "tested the waters" before touching you, just to see if he might be able to get away with it.

Most abuse does not occur at the hand of some stranger lurking in the bushes, awaiting an unknown victim. In some ways the circumstances would be easier to deal with if that were the case, and there are exceptions in which a stranger whisks a little girl away and rapes her. But the majority of sexual abuse is done by someone whom the child knows and probably trusts.

Often the abuser is someone the child cares about, loves, respects, and wishes to please. In most cases molestation is done by close relatives or friends. Your perpetrator may have been (in order of statistical frequency) your father, stepfather, grandparent, uncle, neighbor, brother, family friend, business associate, older playmate, teacher, clergy person—or a complete stranger.

But the question remains: Why you? Let's explore some potential reasons.

POSSIBLE REASONS FOR YOUR SELECTION

Some Men Will Use Anyone/Anything

Some men are willing to use any person they can for their own sexual gratification—even children. A perpetrator has some very serious personality dysfunctions and compulsions that drive him to acts that are immoral, damaging, and criminal. Some males prefer children as sexual partners rather than adults, for reasons we'll explore in a later chapter.

Stop and reflect for a moment. If you were a sexual abuse victim, your rights were denied in a manner that was against the law. You were violated by a male driven by compulsive, deviant behavior. Do you believe this? Or are you still defending your abuser as someone who just couldn't help himself?

You Were a Child

You were somewhat vulnerable, helpless. Perpetrators generally do not seek out adult women of status or power. Rather, they seek out children or women who have less power than they. You were such a person. You didn't have the adult vocabulary to express your objections or the adult power to defend yourself.

The Abuser Was Able to Isolate You

There are lots of little girls in the world, all of whom are pretty and vulnerable. But you were available. For some reason the perpetrator knew that he could coerce (manipulate, threaten, intimidate, and so on) you into not telling on him. Or perhaps he knew that nobody would come to your rescue if you did tell. You were unprotected, rather like unguarded candy in a candy shop. You were there for the taking.

In some way your abuser knew that he could use you and that what he did to you would remain a secret. Perpetrators need secrets. Often they include their victims in the secret, as if it is their secret only. Other perpetrators threaten severe violence to the child or to her pets, parents, and so on. Somehow you were available, unguarded, isolated, or isolat*able*.

You Were Unprotected by Informed Adults

It is likely that you were emotionally unsupported by your mother or father or both. That lack of connection or support set you up as emotionally needy. Your abuser saw that you were low on emotional support. He probably interpreted your vulnerability as your being available to him so that he could use you sexually.

Think about it for a moment. Little girls who have the open love and affection of both their mother and father are usually quite emotionally filled. They don't need a lot of extra love. So they generally do not communicate a receptivity for the inappropriate advances of other people.

When children are vulnerable, unprotected, and needy, a perpetrator tunes in to this and becomes alert, like a predator. He figures he can separate you from the support of your parents, who are in some way absent. Thus you did not seduce him; you did not ask for the abuse; and you are not responsible for what happened. Like a young sheep culled out of a herd by a skilled predator, you were isolated from help and then abused.

The fact that perpetrators, because of their own needs and desires, are able to "read" and isolate victims does not mean that their victims are sexually open to them. Victims are children. Perpetrators are usually adults. Whether your perpetrator interpreted your vulnerability and openness as being sexual openness is irrelevant. He probably saw what he wanted to see and made his plans.

Some theorists say that most human communication is nonverbal. In fact, some say that between 60 and 90 percent of all human interpersonal communication is nonverbal. If this is true, little girls who are somewhat emotionally needy or unsupported probably send out "vibes" that are perceived by others. What others choose to do about these "vibes" is a critical issue. A loving, caring adult man may hug a little girl, tell her she's wonderful, put a kiss on her head, and send her on her way. A perpetrator will fondle her.

You Were Not Well Defended by Your Parents

You probably didn't have the ability to openly go to Mom and Dad and talk about what happened. When most little girls are hurt in any way, they run immediately to Mother or Father and tell the whole story. If the wound is serious or grievous, Mother and Father talk about it together as a team. Then Mother and Father take appropriate action to vindicate the child's honor, to punish the offender, and to protect the child from further harm.

But you, more than likely, were somehow separated from that process of open communication, vindication, and protection. And somehow your perpetrator figured it out. Perhaps he caused it to happen. Abusers are predatory, looking for and sizing up the most vulnerable prey and then plotting moves to bring about their plans.

Children Are Taught to Be Compliant

Little girls are usually taught from infancy to be compliant and to obey adults. Little girls are not supposed to stand up and fight. Instead, they are supposed to be protected. In fact, within this culture little girls are frequently given less latitude for overt disobedience of adults than are little boys.

Little Girls Have Greater Relational Vulnerability

The field of developmental psychology asserts that little girls develop along more relational "tracks" than do little boys (Piaget,

1965). Little boys tend to obtain much of their sense of identity through competition using rules and structure (for example, playing baseball and football). Little girls, on the other hand, obtain much of their sense of identity through more relational activities (for example, playing "house" and "dolls"). In recent work Carol Gilligan (1982) validates and elaborates on this.

This is not to say that little boys don't need to be held and loved by their mothers and fathers. But girls tend more often to end up in the arms of some person who wishes to give them some loving. And if this person is an abuser, then he has set the stage.

LOVE GIVEN VERSUS LOVE RECEIVED

It is important to note that there is a difference between a parent's love for a child and the child's knowledge of that love. Some parents love their children deeply, yet are not able to communicate this love to the children. Sometimes children know intellectually that they are loved, but they do not feel the emotional connection with that love.

On the other hand, some parents don't care much for their kids. Perhaps there are other matters drawing the parent's energy away from the child—a shaky marriage, a demanding job, financial difficulties, low parental self-esteem, an affair, a parent's own childhood abuse. There are a host of reasons why some parents don't pour themselves into their children. When a parent doesn't effectively communicate love for a child, the child often responds to that loss by being more receptive to other adults' love—genuine or not. This often sets the stage for abuse.

THE STAGE IS OFTEN SET AT AN EARLY AGE

Generally speaking, the earlier in the child's development that the mother/child relationship is damaged in any way, the more pervasive the damage is within the child. If there is little or no close mother/child interaction during the child's first year of life, the damage will likely be deeper and more pervasive than if the relationship is wounded during the child's second year.

This lack is not usually something that the child can remember consciously. It is usually carried forward into adulthood in the form of feelings: loneliness, emptiness, a vague sense of loss or abandonment, perhaps restlessness. But if Mom is emotionally or physically unavailable to the child during the first few years of life, a seed of emotional deficit is already planted in the child. This deficit may produce a sense of emotional neediness or vulnerability in the child in later years.

As the child grows from infant to toddler, Mother too goes through her own stages. As the child begins to walk and talk, a natural process of becoming separate (called *separation/individuation*) occurs. The child begins to become her little self, separate from Mother.

Some mothers view this separation as a loss. Other mothers feel relief in that they can quit giving so much time and energy to the child. In either case, if the mother uses this stage as an opportunity to disconnect from the child, the child will feel the lack of emotional closeness. Again, this can be a seed, probably affecting the child even more in later life.

The next stage in normal child development occurs around age three, when the child, having toddled around the "world" (the house or the apartment) on her own for a while, now wishes to come back to Mom for a while. This stage is called *rapprochement*, a French word meaning a time of wishing to reattach.

But this time the child is not an infant. She is a small individual. If Mother does not accept the child's desire to come back into the relationship, again the child will feel the emotional distance. That feeling will sink into the child's makeup and may be played out in the child's personality and relationships in the years ahead.

As the child continues to mature, there are other identifiable stages of growth and development. At each stage in the life of a little girl, Mother is key. Father is very important, but for girls the primary relationship between child and adult is between the mother and daughter.

Many types of damage may be done to affect the mother-daughter bond. Mother may be too cold or demanding. She may be too rigid and critical. She may be too busy, too old, or too young and immature for parenting. On the other hand, she may be too syrupy and clingy, which is just another way for some moms to control. Mom may be too quirky, too religious, too Bohemian, too anything. There may be too many children to tend and not enough help. Mom may be too angry at Dad, at her own mother, or at the world in general, and may vent her anger onto her daughter. Mom may be the one responsible for keeping the household together, may be holding down two jobs, may be dead tired much of the time, and may just not have the energy to be a good parent as well.

The point is that if there are damaging aspects of the mother-daughter relationship, especially during the formative years, the child will probably feel the effect in later years. The child may never know why she feels emotionally empty or vulnerable but the feeling is very real and is frequently experienced as the child grows through early childhood into adolescence and arrives at adulthood.

The feeling of loss often positions the child to approach the world with arms extended, proclaiming a nonverbal message: "I am a child who would love to be loved by someone."

This discussion serves to explain why you are not responsible for your abuse. You did not in any way seduce your abuser. Now you have an insight into the type of child who is often selected by adult sexual offenders.

YOUR OWN EMOTIONAL VULNERABILITY

Should a woman trust anyone with her emotional vulnerability? Remember, her "neediness" may have led her into a difficult situation in the past, and she may wish to avoid feelings of shame and anger in the future. The answer to this question is twofold.

First, you have probably become somewhat adept at shielding your own sense of emotional vulnerability from others. This is common in victims. The reason is not too hard to understand. Vulnerability can lead to pain, as in the abusive situation.

In healing, the question you must resolve is how much isolation you can or should live with. Shielding yourself from all forms of emotional or relational vulnerability usually creates interpersonal isolation.

In the healing process, two of your challenges will be to trust another person with your real self and then to accept the fact that you are lovable. The first way to deal with your emotional vulnerability, then, is to risk sharing it with a few carefully selected people who care for you and probably would continue to care for you even if you shared your secret. Give them a chance to know you and love you.

Another challenge involves accepting that you must learn how to fill the void that probably lies inside you. It's not fair, but as an adult you are now left with some damage in your soul. You are the only one who can figure out how to repair it and then how to reconnect with life.

This requires a shift or a major change in life and thought process. To understand this shift, let's use the analogy of a bucket for a moment.

Victims frequently feel as if their bucket is empty. Some victims' buckets only have some muddy water in the bottom; they are not full of the fresh, pure water of life. Victims also frequently feel that their task in life is to keep people from taking any more of their water or from punching any more holes in their buckets. Theirs is both a defensive and a fearful posture.

Functioning people, on the other hand, work at keeping their bucket filled and fresh. If someone throws a handful of mud into the bucket, they work at washing it out.

Victims wait for others to fill their buckets. Victims believe they are not able to fill their own buckets. As a victim, one of your biggest challenges is to learn to fill your own bucket with love and supportive relationships so that you can live with a feeling of acceptance, nurturing, and support.

SUMMARY

So why did your perpetrator choose you? Perhaps it was blind circumstance. Perhaps he saw your vulnerability. Perhaps he knew he could use you without anyone shouting to the world, "Look at what this criminal has done to this little girl!"

He was a criminal. Even if he was your father, at that moment when he molested and violated you, he was a criminal. Whoever he was, that person took advantage of a weaker person. He used you for his sickness.

Perhaps he saw you as needy. But who cares what he saw? The issue for you to focus on is not what you represented to him or how he selected you. Although you were certainly involved in the abuse by being a victim, the selection process is not your issue. It's his. Is the money in a bank responsible for the bank robber coming to steal it? Is the jewelry in a lady's dresser responsible for the burglar who comes to rob it? Neither is the girl responsible for the adult who robs and steals her self-esteem, her innocence, and her girlhood dreams of simple purity.

The jury comes into the courtroom. You watch as the jury foreman turns to the judge and says, "We find the little girl innocent. She deserves restitution. We find the perpetrator guilty. We don't care why he chose to commit the act. What he did was wrong, and he deserves punishment." The judge bangs his gavel and says, "This court finds the perpetrator guilty on all counts, and the victim innocent."

QUESTIONS FOR REFLECTION

1. Reflect upon your own childhood. What emotional feelings do you have about your relationship with your mother? Were you strongly supported by and emotionally close to her? Or was there some distance or some barrier across which you could not or would not pass?

2. Reflect upon the age(s) at which you were abused. How was your personal vulnerability communicated to the perpetrator? How did he know he could use you and you wouldn't "blow the whistle" on him? How did he isolate you from help?

3. Reflect upon your own sense of "attachment hunger" and how it developed. Is there any connection between what you desired in a normal, healthy relationship and how the perpetrator used that desire for his purposes?

4. Reflect upon whether you really believe that you were not responsible for your abuse. Do you still have a sense of being responsible? As you think about this, check your feelings as compared to your mind's response. Is there a difference? You may cognitively respond that you were not responsible, yet carry feelings that you were. Why might this conflict exist between the two?

═══ *ACTION ITEMS* ═══

1. Find a place where you can be alone for at least an hour, where nobody will see you, no phones will ring, and no one will

interrupt you. Then, in your mind's eye, face the person(s) who abused you one at a time. Create a mental picture in which you are protected against anything they may say to you. Tell them individually that they did not have your permission to abuse you. Tell them that what they did was not OK. Tell them that they are evil and deviant. Tell them that they hurt you more than they'll ever realize.

Write what you would say to your abuser(s).

2. Visualize yourself in a courtroom. You have just told the world what your abuser(s) did to you. This courtroom is a safe environment in which you can be completely honest. Now the whole secret is out in the open. You are relieved to have told the whole story, and the jurors wept as they listened to you. You sense their feelings of sadness on your behalf and their anger at your abuser(s).

Now it's time for the abuser(s) to stand and try to offer a defense. What will your perpetrator(s) say? How will they try to defend their actions? Will they talk about their own needs and how they used you to gratify themselves? Will they talk about your powerlessness and vulnerability? Will they try to make the jury believe that you wanted to be abused? Will they tell the jury that you seduced them? Listen to your abuser(s) stammer, and watch them shift their weight from one foot to the other as they try to make the crime appear reasonable.

They can't do it! The jury is enraged! Look at the faces of the jury!

Write down what you think your abuser(s) would say, and write down what you believe the jury would be thinking as your abuser(s) attempted to make a case.

3. Visualize reporters now, waiting for the story. What will they write? Will they say that you were a seductive and evil little girl, or will they write about the sick and evil man who abused you? (If you have any doubt at all, pick up a newspaper and read what reporters write about child abuse.)

Now the story is out. It's in all the papers. And it says, "You were victimized! You are not guilty! You have nothing to be ashamed of! You were abused! The abuser was the sick one!"

Write that newspaper article.

FOR SPIRITUAL GROWTH

1. Psalms 22:9–10 and 71:5–6 speak of God bringing us from the womb into life. He is portrayed as knowing us intimately from

the very beginning. Is it possible that in the midst of our pain God is there beside us, from birth until death? If God does not intervene and stop bad people from abusing us, what can be the purpose or benefit of His presence with us through it all?

2. Psalm 46:10 says, "Cease striving and know that I am God" (NASB). Another translation says, "Be still, and know that I am God" (NKJV). Ponder what it might be like to put the whole world on hold and spend a little time focusing on God—believing that He is there, that He loves you, that He grieves when you are wounded. You may wish to ask Him if you may walk close beside Him for the rest of your life.

3. Psalm 23:4 says, "Even though I walk through the valley of the shadow of death, / I fear no evil; / for thou art with me" (RSV). David was not speaking of actual death in this verse, but rather "the valley of the shadow" of it—deep hurt, deep fear, possibly heavy depression. As you walk through your hurt, consider that God is walking beside you, just as David knew that God was walking close beside him.

4. Psalm 34:18 says, "The LORD is close to the brokenhearted / and saves those who are crushed in spirit" (NIV). Again, the theme is that of the nearness of God in the midst of our pain. What could this text mean in your life as you move toward recovery?

Chapter 5
Lies!

Sexual abuse victims have usually lived within a system of distortions and deceptions. We asked one of our recovery groups to give us some examples from their own lives. If you're a victim, compare these distortions and deceptions with yours. (Some items have been slightly modified, with personal names deleted and/or personal touches made more generic.)

DECEPTIONS AND DISTORTIONS
VICTIMS HEAR

This section contains actual lies told to victims, either by perpetrators or by mothers who lived in denial. Then one or two implications behind each lie will be suggested.

1. "You and your brother are troublemakers, disturbance

breeders!" *Implication:* You and your brother are responsible for your problems. Parents don't want to hear or know the truth.

2. "You slut! You're a dirty little slut!" *Implication:* You are dirty and evil. *Possible further implication:* Therefore, I (the abuser) am justified in sexually abusing you.

3. "You're just letting your imagination carry you away." *Implication:* If I (the parent) deny the validity of what you're telling me, it will go away.

4. "Just turn all your problems over to the Lord and let Him take care of them." *Implication:* Spiritualize your problems and they'll disappear. (This is a common form of denial, sometimes called *religious denial*.)

5. "You're so lazy!" *Implication:* Therefore, I am justified in abusing you.

6. "I knew you'd be back to apologize." *Implication:* You were wrong in leaving me. I knew you'd buckle under my pressure and come back to me. (Note the power play. This is common in ongoing abuse.)

7. "Your conscience gives you a worse whipping than I ever could." *Implication:* Abuse victims deserve punishment rather than love, nurturing, and defense against the abuser.

8. "You're dumb! You're so stupid!" *Implication:* That's what I'll tell you so you'll believe I have the right to "teach" you—a common excuse for many forms of child abuse.

9. "You don't love me." *Implication:* If you did, you'd let me abuse you.

10. "Wearing short pants is a sin against God!" *Implication:* You were seductive; you sinned against God by wearing certain clothing.

11. "Bright-colored clothes are too flashy and unbecoming for a child of God." *Implication:* You are responsible for your abuse because you dressed seductively. God got even with you by having you sexually abused.

12. "Cutting and curling your hair is sinful." *Implication:* You were responsible for your abuse because you did your hair a certain way.

13. "We must think of ourselves as the lowest of the low before God will really accept us. We're just the dust of the earth, worth little, if anything, in God's sight." *Implication:* God wants us to both

act and think like victims. We're worthless. (Incidentally, this is absolutely not the case. Christ's willingness to die on the cross demonstrates the greatest possible love for us. God values us dearly!)

14. "God loves us. That's why it's necessary for Him to use such harsh methods of teaching His children." *Implication:* Sexual abuse is a form of God's love. *Further implication:* Pain equals love.

15. "My harshness means I love you." *Implication:* The more I hurt you, the more I show how much I love you. (Note: It's easy to see where distorted thinking comes from, isn't it!)

16. "You're too maladjusted to hold down any job except baby-sitting. You're too nervous to safely drive a car." *Implication:* I need to "help" you by lowering your self-esteem so that you'll stay in servitude to and dependence upon me.

17. "You're big for your age." *Implication:* You need me to show you what's in store for you.

18. "You're sloppy and messy." *Implication:* Therefore, it's OK for me to abuse you.

19. "You're too emotional. You wear your heart on your sleeve." *Implication:* Your feelings don't count; ignore them. My feelings are the only ones that count.

20. "You're just like your mother." *Implication:* Mother was a victim, so you should be one too.

21. "I don't have anybody with me any longer. You owe me after all I've given you." (Presumably spoken by a perpetrating father whose wife died.) *Implication:* Perpetrator's sexual needs are more important than victim's social, emotional, and spiritual well-being and more important than truth and integrity.

22. "Your father loves you." *Implication:* Sexual abuse is a form of love.

23. "Our family was normal and natural because we had dinner together every night." *Implication:* Dinner at 6:00 negates the horror of sexual abuse at 11:00.

24. "If I didn't have you, I'd kill myself." *Implication:* You, the victim, are responsible for my life. If you don't let me use you, then you will be blamed for my suicide.

25. "I'll always love you, and I will never leave you." *Implication:* Sexual abuse equals love. *Further implication:* Because I am sexually out of control and will never choose to leave you, you have the

same responsibility to me. *Further implication:* I will never stop using you as a victim as long as you allow it.

26. "I'll be there if you ever need me." *Implication:* Because I'm out of control and available for you, you should be available for me.

27. "Tell me everything, darling; we're so close." *Implication:* Emotional voyeurism can be stimulating to me (your abuser), and it might lead to sexual activity too. So I'll listen to you in return for your "favors."

28. "You are unattractive." *Implication:* If I (the abuser) can make you feel bad enough about yourself, then I can "rescue" you by providing sexual attention. I can also control you and keep you from leaving me by taking away your hope of ever feeling attractive enough to have a normal, healthy relationship.

29. "Why couldn't you have been like your sisters?" *Implication:* You're not as good as they are; in fact, you're not worthy of healthy relationships.

30. "You *should* have known better; you *should* have stopped him (the abuser)!" (Probably spoken by a mother in deep denial herself.) *Implication:* Because you didn't stop him, you must have wanted to be abused. *Further implication:* You had the power to stop him.

31. "If you tell anyone, the family will fall apart, and it will be your fault." *Implication:* Victims are responsible for maintaining the family system, its secrets, and its disease.

32. "If you tell anyone I'll kill the family." *Implication:* Death of family will be victim's responsibility rather than perpetrator's choice.

33. "It's all in the past. Why bring it up again?" *Implication:* Leaving sexual abuse in the past makes it go away. Ignoring truth is better than facing it. *Further implication:* You're immature or unstable or wrong for not leaving it in the past.

34. "You imagined it!" *Implication:* Don't trust your memory or your feelings. Doubt yourself.

35. "You chose to live like you are, so you should be treated like scum." *Implication:* Victims deserve to be treated like scum.

36. "You're so homely, with that long stringy hair." *Implication:* Nobody will ever want you. I (the abuser) may be your only chance to have a sexual relationship.

37. "You killed your father; you made your mother crazy!"

Implication: Victims are responsible for the choices, lives, and mental health of perpetrators and/or other sick family members.

38. "I have to teach you something about sex." *Implication:* Perpetrators are doing the right thing by sexually abusing victims. *Further implication:* Victims are incapable of learning about sexuality when they reach adulthood.

39. "If you tell, you'll be in trouble!" *Implication:* You'll be harmed if you go for help. (A common technique used by abusers to isolate victims from help.)

40. "Don't tell me anything, *I know!*" (Spoken by abuser.) *Implication:* Perpetrators know all; victims know nothing. Just shut up and do what I tell you to do.

41. "You wanted it." *Implication:* Victims enjoy abuse.

42. "You deserved it." *Implication:* Victims deserve abuse.

43. "Your dad will be disappointed in you if you tell him what you've been doing." (Spoken by victim's mother.) *Implication:* Sexual abuse is victim's fault and responsibility. *Further implication:* Victim is separated from the love, help, support, and healing of Mother *and* Father.

44. "This happens to lots of people! Women use this as an excuse for everything." *Implication:* Sexual abuse is normal. *Further implication:* To claim sexual abuse is to make excuses for one's own "chosen" sexual activity.

45. "You're going to have to control yourself." *Implication:* Sexual abuse is a matter of personal choice. Therefore, personal control is an option.

46. "Nothing was wrong." *Implication:* Your having been abused was not wrong. It was right and normal. *Further implication:* Don't trust your own feelings.

47. "It was just play." *Implication:* It's OK to use play as an excuse for sexually abusing a child.

48. "I did not do that to you and you know it!" *Implication:* If perpetrator puts enough direct pressure on victim, perpetrator can make victim mistrust her memory. (Note: Aggressive denial is a very difficult hurdle to overcome. Almost all perpetrators overtly deny that they ever sexually abused anyone.)

49. "You consented to it!" *Implication:* If a perpetrator can manipulate a child to nonresistance of abuse, then it's OK to abuse.

50. "Boy, what a figure!" *Implication:* Because you have a good figure, I (the abuser) have a right to use it.

51. "You can't take care of yourself." *Implication:* You need me to "help" you.

LIES VICTIMS TELL THEMSELVES

As a result of living in an atmosphere of distortions and deception, victims learn to adopt many lies as truth. Victims often live with a highly distorted self-perception. Following are some of the victim self-messages from the women in one of our recovery groups.

1. I'm dumb, stupid, and unintelligent.
2. I'm abnormal.
3. I must walk the chalk line or God will blast me.
4. I can't make good decisions.
5. I'm dull.
6. I must protect my brothers and sisters from being injured or harmed.
7. My very being is unnatural because my father was unnatural.
8. I'm unlovable.
9. I'll never be loved or married.
10. If I'm not perfect, I'm nothing.
11. Maybe I was not really abused. Perhaps my memory's wrong.
12. I wasn't abused as badly as other victims. (*Implication:* Therefore, my abuse is not significant.)
13. I am unattractive.
14. I should have had more self-confidence.
15. I cannot relate to men.
16. I have messed up my life with the choices I have made.
17. I probably deserve bad treatment.
18. If I let you in, you'll find out I'm no good.
19. I'm better off alone. Then I won't bother anyone.
20. I'm always in the way, making someone angry.
21. If someone is upset it's probably my fault.
22. I'm fat and ugly.
23. Nobody could ever like me.
24. I'm strange.

25. I deserve everything that happens to me.
26. I'm unforgivable.
27. I could have stopped it.
28. I'm lazy.
29. I'm incapable of having a healthy relationship.
30. It's dangerous to let yourself feel.
31. Walk away when it hurts.
32. It's not OK to ask for what you need.
33. Ignore pain.
34. I asked for it by not telling him to leave me alone.
35. I must have enjoyed it or I'd have asked him to stop.
36. I'm damaged and can never be the same again.
37. It's not important. I'm not important.
38. It doesn't affect me. I can handle it.
39. I'm dirty.
40. I'm irreversibly stained.
41. I led him on.
42. I can never trust women.
43. I'm making too big a deal about all of this.
44. I'm oversensitive.
45. I shouldn't cry about this. Something is wrong with me.
46. I'm a bad person.
47. I'm fat.
48. I'm only good for sex.
49. It was all my fault that I didn't enjoy it.
50. Something is deeply wrong with me.
51. I'm not going to make it in life.
52. It didn't happen. I'm just crazy. I can't believe myself.
53. Just forgive. Jesus said that if we forgive, it'll all go away.
54. I'm lying.
55. I consented to it by not fighting.
56. I've done what is unforgivable in the eyes of God.
57. I am a mistake.
58. I can't take care of myself.
59. If anyone gets too close to me he won't like me.
60. He couldn't help himself; I was overdeveloped at an early age.
61. I am ruined for life.
62. Nobody could want to marry someone as dirty as I am.

63. I must be perfect to be loved.

64. He didn't mean to hurt me.

Do you see the repetitive themes in these statements? Can you see the wreckage in the lives of these women as they describe their inner selves? Doesn't it make you want to cry? These human beings are struggling with all their souls just to cope. Can you see that what happened long ago is still alive and painful?

If you're a victim, many of those self-talk messages may seem normal. If this is true for you, you may need help in sorting out deception from truth.

POSITIVE SELF-TALK

We've spent time reflecting on deceptions and distortions. In our lives there is also the potential for truth and goodness. Following are some true messages given by *the same group* of victims as they began to perceive the deceptions and distortions with which they had been living; as they began to see some of the truth; as they began to trust their own thinking and feeling abilities; and as they began to recognize some of their own good qualities.

1. I'm a neat, clean, hardworking person.

2. I'm a peacemaker.

3. I'm a sweet person, a woman.

4. I know this is real (the abuse); it actually happened to me.

5. God will help me heal.

6. I did nothing wrong. I was a child.

7. Getting angry is fine. Dad should have been the one apologizing.

8. I'm smart.

9. I have good common sense, and I use it well.

10. I have a lovely voice.

11. They (the family) can handle it (if I tell the truth).

12. I'm attractively shaped and even slim.

13. I'm beautiful.

14. I speak intelligently.

15. What I say is a good contribution to the conversation.

16. I'm a very caring person.

17. My manners are very good, and I'm proud to be polite.

18. My (own) family is my priority (as compared with the family of origin: mother/father/siblings).

19. I am very unselfish, and I am a compassionate person.

20. I am very likable.

21. I am honest about my feelings.

22. I can allow myself to remember.

23. I'm just as good as anybody else.

24. I am very normal.

25. Though I have been basically an angry person, I can and will change into a vibrantly happy and healed person.

26. PMS sometimes accelerates my anger—it's not just an excuse.

27. I love my husband and would never deliberately hurt anyone I love.

28. I can love other people, and I can be loved too!

29. God doesn't care about my clothing. It's me He loves.

30. I love bright, flashy colors, and I believe God does too!

31. God is gentle; I can trust Him. I can give myself to Him.

32. God wants me to be comfortable and to look attractive.

33. I'm worth everything to God. He wants me to have a good self-image.

34. God is gentle and patient because He loves me. He is not harsh.

35. Gentleness and patience equal love.

36. I can do any job I choose.

37. I can trust my husband.

38. I'm just the right size and shape for me.

39. I always try my best.

40. I have a mind and a heart, and both are healthy.

41. My father wasn't capable of mature, unconditional love.

42. I'm just like me. I may have some characteristics of my mother, but if I don't like them I can change.

43. God is my Creator, not my (physical) father. (This victim was separating God the Father from the image of her own physical father, who abused her.)

44. I was a kid! Don't lay (adult) responsibility on me!

45. I'm very lovable.

46. I may find someone to marry; I may not. Either way I'm OK.

47. Who *wants* to be perfect?

48. I can celebrate my humanness.

49. I was abused differently (than other victims may have been). Still, I was very abused.

50. People leave. Sometimes people were never really there. I can't lose what I never had.

51. My abuser was irresponsible.

52. I am clean.

53. I am a pure, whole woman.

54. I am a good person.

55. I didn't lead them (the perpetrators) on.

56. I am not overly agitated. I am accurate.

57. I am empathic and warmhearted. I listen to my feelings.

58. I am a sensitive person.

59. It's OK to cry.

60. Nothing, absolutely nothing, is wrong with me.

61. I am a slender, attractive woman.

62. I am good for all things in life.

63. I don't have to enjoy abuse.

64. I am making it in life—without a man!

65. I am sane.

66. It did happen to me.

67. I tell the truth.

68. I don't have to forgive (just) in order to please people.

69. I can choose to forgive when I am ready.

70. It's OK to get help.

71. I believe God has forgiven me.

72. I deserve to be treated well.

73. I deserve to be pampered.

74. I deserve to be loved.

75. I have a beautiful nose and face.

76. God gave me my face.

77. I have a beautiful figure.

78. I did not consent to the abuse. It happened.

79. I'm intelligent.

80. I'm whole.

81. I have a beautiful chest.

82. I am taking care of myself.

83. If you get close to me, you're really, really going to like me.

84. I like myself.

85. My body is just fine the way it is.

86. It's OK to be pretty and thin. It's not a sin.

87. I am not my parents. I choose to be different.

88. I can forgive myself.

89. Not everyone considers me defective.

90. I am not my sisters.

91. I could not stop the abuse.

92. I do have more confidence. I am working on it.

93. The family would not have fallen apart (if I had told).

94. I am growing and developing my confidence—a task that my parents should have begun.

95. I am acting as my own parent to "protect" myself.

96. The family would not have been killed (if I had told).

97. I can relate to men.

98. I can be happy with what makes me happy.

99. I did not imagine it (the abuse).

100. I made the choices I did, good and bad, in the best way I knew how, in order to survive.

101. I didn't say no, but the circumstances made my decision for me.

102. I have a lot to offer someone.

103. I do count!

104. I am not homely.

105. I will amount to anything I want to.

106. I can do things I really want to do.

107. I have done very well on my own.

108. I did not kill my father.

109. I did not make my mother crazy.

110. I am not stupid. I have a 3.75 grade point average.

111. I was too young to be "taught" about sex.

112. If I had told, he would have been the one in trouble. He isolated me so I wouldn't tell.

113. He was very insecure and had to be the ruler.

114. I'm in charge of myself.

115. I'm pretty! I'm really pretty!

116. I do not deserve to be treated badly; I deserve to be treated as a lady.

117. I am lovable, caring, and giving.

118. I need more roses!

119. I don't bother anyone. All persons need to take care of themselves.

120. I'm not in the way.

121. It was not my fault.

122. I can't take care of everyone.

123. I live a good life, and I have strong morals.

124. I did not deserve it. I was a child who knew nothing about sex until he showed me what it was and how to do sexual things with other guys.

125. My dad would not have been disappointed in me. He would have shot him (the perpetrator). He would have protected me.

126. It's OK for me to be "out of control" if I want to be.

127. It (the abuse) was not "play." Children do not play that way.

128. I was raped.

129. There is more to sexuality than wearing adult underwear.

130. It's OK to allow myself to feel and to take care of myself.

131. I was hurting, but Mom and Dad couldn't see it.

132. If someone hurts me, I can tell him to stop!

133. I don't use chocolate (or food in general) to make me feel better now.

134. I can wear pretty things that fit. I can look attractive because I have my spirit back.

OTHER THOUGHTS FROM VICTIMS

The following thoughts were contributed by women who are processing some of the troubling thoughts that can plague victims.

1. "I did have sex with men and women. I tried to correct the situation by sex, but it didn't work. I have been victimized. I am dealing with my molestation and rape, even though it is difficult, scary, and sad."

2. "So what if it happened to a lot of girls. It should never have happened to anyone. It should never have happened to me. Women deserve understanding and help dealing with this. It's degrading, humiliating. Abuse robs a child of her innocence and spirit. It teaches a child that sex is OK and perhaps the norm, when in reality it (the abuse) is *not* normal."

3. "It (the abuse) is wrong. Family members do not have sex with one another."

4. "I was an early developer, and my brothers raped me. I wanted to die. I wanted to cut off my breasts so that they wouldn't use me any more. I still think about cutting them off. God help me not to cut off my breasts."

5. "I didn't know what was going on. I felt extremely confused and scared; yet when he was rubbing me I felt turned on. I didn't know what that phrase meant. I felt stimulated. For a few years I wondered if I enjoyed it. But now I look back on it and wish I could change everything."

Every victim has her own story, and each one is a new chapter in horror, humiliation, shame, confusion, emotional trauma, sadness, and wretchedness. If one hundred victims told their stories, we would hear about one hundred different methods of abuse.

Victims live with a complex network of distortion and deception. These deceptions are not just little white lies; they are evil manipulations told by abusers and others who need the denial inherent in abuse. It is no wonder, then, that the world of the victim is often so confusing. How could anyone make sense of a world so filled with deceit and distortion?

As one of the women wrote her list of positive messages, she also wrote two comments in the margins. First she wrote, "Painful." Second she wrote, "I write these but I don't truly believe all of them. It's hard for me to like me." As this victim has pursued healing, her belief in the truth and her hope for her own future are slowly but very surely becoming bright and positive.

REFRAMING THE PICTURE

Read through the section on positive self-talk again. See how the victims had to work at changing their reality? That's what you need to do—to change the way you see your world.

Let's call this exercise *reframing*. Imagine a picture. It's a lovely picture with flowers, sunlight, and a lake. A lively, gentle lady graces the middle of the picture. She's sitting on a blanket with a delightful picnic basket, and she's reading her favorite book. She is wearing a lovely pastel summer outfit, comfortable and cool. She has braided field flowers into her hair.

Now imagine this picture placed in an ugly, horrid, greasy, smelly frame. The frame is so bad that it ruins the picture. The frame is huge—imposing. It's brutish and is held together with rough nails, barbed wire, and twine.

Visualize your life as the picture. Your circumstances built the frame. It's OK—in fact, it's appropriate and necessary—for you to reframe your picture. This reframing requires that you strip off the old frame—that ugly piece of trash that convinced you that you, too, were trash.

Now imagine looking at the picture set in another frame. The new frame is delicate, a soft shade of white with pink highlights. It's made of the finest wood and is well glued and sturdy. It reminds you of simplicity, purity, and all things lovely. Looking at the picture in this frame makes you happy.

Getting rid of the deceptions and distortions in your life is like taking off the old frame and burning it. Go ahead! Do it! For your own happiness, for your emotional and spiritual health, for your future, destroy the old frame. Build a new one.

It's your picture, your life. You can believe what you want to believe about yourself. As you change what you believe about yourself, as you discard the old frame and put on the new one, you will find yourself looking differently at the picture. This is appropriate and good.

And then, *for the rest of your life, anytime* you catch yourself looking at the picture in the old frame, take the frame off, smash it, burn it, and throw the ashes into the sea. Destroy it. Do it as often as necessary. You are not what they told you. You are what you tell yourself you are. Perhaps of greatest value, you are what God tells you: lovely, pure, whole, forgiven, and of great value. You are precious.

Read what the Bible says: "For if a [woman] is in Christ, [she] becomes a new person altogether—the past is *finished and gone,* everything has become *fresh and new*" (2 Cor. 5:17 PHILLIPS, italics added). This is another reason that God's Word contains good news. God can help reframe the picture, no matter how ugly the old frame was.

This is not done by using smoke and mirrors. It's not done by becoming perfect and thereby pleasing God. It's done simply by saying, "God, I don't want to live like this anymore. Please take away the burden of the junk and the pain in my life. I want so much to give it all to You. Please begin lifting my load, and fill me with Your Spirit. Please make me whole again. Pure again. Lovely again. Fresh again. Lord, please come into my life as only You can, and help me clean house. Pour Your healing salve upon my cuts. God, in Your eyes and in my eyes, please restore me. I want a new frame."

In Christ's death sin, pain, evil, and brokenness were nailed to the cross and forgiven forever. After the Cross came the Resurrection—new life, even after death; wholeness after being defiled; healing after suffering; joy after sorrow.

No matter how long it takes or how scary or sad the process becomes, commit yourself to reframing your picture. Commit yourself to God too, because He's a wonderful artist and healer.

QUESTIONS FOR REFLECTION

1. Name three or four effects that distortions and deceptions have upon victims. Think about issues such as isolation, destruction of self-esteem, and control. How did these issues gain their own strength by the use of distortions and deceptions? What names did the perpetrator call you to demean you and make you more pliable for his use? What are some other issues that apply to your experiences?

2. Who were the primary perpetrators of distortions and deceptions in your abuse?

3. Why are children so susceptible to believing distortions and deceptions?

4. Why are distortions and deceptions essential for abuse to continue?

5. How would knowing the truth have changed your life at the time of your abuse? How can it change your life now?

═══ ACTION ITEMS ═══

1. Make three long lists of your own, using several pages each. Entitle List 1 "Distortions and deceptions I was told by my family and/or perpetrator(s)." Head List 2 "Distortions and deceptions I have told myself." List 3 should contain the truth about these distortions and deceptions.

2. Make a pretty frame for yourself out of paper, wood, or anything you wish. Or you may go to a store and buy a lovely one. Hang your beautiful frame on the wall where you can see it daily, and visualize your own lovely picture in it. Every time you start hearing, believing, or acting upon any of the lies of your life, go to the frame and visualize God's healing truth and His love. Use this tool to change the way you see your world, the way you see yourself, and the way you react to yourself and to all of your relationships.

FOR SPIRITUAL GROWTH

1. Read Romans 8:1–2. Then reflect upon this question: Is there *any* condemnation God holds against us for *any* reason?

2. Read Luke 7:36–50. This woman had, in her own mind, cried out, "Enough! I don't want to live like this any longer!" To whom did she turn? Notice the circumstances and who (besides Christ) was in the room. Read how Christ defended her. Put yourself in that room, in her place, and meditate upon His defending you.

3. Memorize 2 Corinthians 5:17, using the word *woman* rather than *man*.

Chapter 6
Looking for Your Mother and Your Child

A few years ago I was visiting some friends. Their four-year-old daughter came running into the house and exclaimed, "Billy wants me to pull down my pants so he can look at me. Is that OK?" She was checking with Mommy; and of course, Mommy said that wasn't a good idea. Then Daddy went outside looking for Billy, and I suspect that at some point Daddy had a short discussion with Billy's parents. That's as it should be. Both parents should act as a network backing up their children, protecting if necessary, and listening to their children's questions and comments.

Little girls who are sexually abused often don't have access to Mother; and sometimes it's Father doing the abusing. In another chapter we'll expand on this separation of mother from daughter. The focus of this chapter is the long-term effect this separation often has upon women when they reach adulthood.

One victim (we'll call her Stephanie) has been grieving the loss of her mother. Her mother died when Stephanie was a baby. One might ask why, at her age, she still keenly feels the loss of her mom. This factor is deeper than it may appear and is important to understand.

When a little girl has a good, healthy, open, communicative relationship with a healthy mother, she has the comfort of knowing not only that she is loved, but also that no matter what may happen to her, Mom is there—both as a resource and a source of protection. In a traditional two-parent home, she and Mom also have Dad as a solid source of protection.

But to a little girl, the key relationship is usually with Mom. When a young girl of any age is sexually assaulted, it is normal for her to turn to her mother.

The reasons Mother may not be available are many. Sometimes Mom is mentally or physically ill. Sometimes Mom is a crabby, distant person. Sometimes she has died. But the fact that Mom is not available represents a major breach in what *should be*. This unavailability represents a critical vacuum in the life and fledgling relationships of a child. This problem is not confined to girls subjected to sexual abuse. The absence of Mom's availability usually represents a larger issue of a mother who is "not there" for the girl in many other ways as well.

Many abuse victims speak of grieving for a mother who never really loved them. Even if Mom was in the home, for some reason she was not the type of person or didn't have the time, ability, or inclination to prepare her daughter for life the way daughters need Mom to do. This is often a grievous loss, meaning not only the absence of protection from sexual abuse. It also represents the loss of a deep and enduring mother-daughter friendship that normally sustains many women through life's most difficult ordeals. Deeper still, this separation often leads to the loss of part of a woman's self-identity.

Replacing Mom is impossible. We only have one mother. However, there are two avenues of help open to women who are abuse victims.

SURROGATE MOTHER

It may seem foolish for a grown woman to seek a surrogate mom—someone willing to show motherly qualities to a woman whose own mother was unavailable. Yet among women this type of relationship is not at all unusual.

One most be selective in this process, but probably everyone knows at least one woman who has "adopted" another, either as her child or her mother. Sometimes this adoption process is openly spoken of, and at other times it's demonstrated only. Either way, this "substitution" can be a powerful tool for one's healing.

Sharing with another woman can be tremendously healing, particularly with a woman who may in some ways fit one's idea of a surrogate mother. To see "Mom's" eyes well up with tears in hearing the agonies of the abuse; to feel her anger against the abuser; to lose oneself in her arms and just cry for a while; and to know that she still loves you, no matter what, can effect great healing and bring a perspective of peace to past memories.

Pride is the quality that usually prevents a victim from having this type of experience. "Oh, I couldn't do that to another woman." Having a loving, nurturing relationship with another person is not something "done to" that person. Sharing one's soul with another person does not draw from one's relational "bank"; it adds immensely to it.

When we share ourselves openly, in genuine, warm relationships, we usually wind up being nurtured. And the other person has a sense of fulfilling God's purpose in creating her—to offer the love of God to another person.

ONESELF AS MOTHER

The other format for "mother substitution" has the potential of being equally profound. It involves a journey backward in time, both as adult and child. It's called "going back for the child." Simply put, it involves you going back in your memories to make a loving, caring, nurturing connection with yourself when you were a child. Hold that child; forgive her if needed; encourage her; explain that she is not a bad girl even if she thinks she is; and protect her.

Step 1

First, find a comfortable chair or a sofa on which you can sit and dream. Then close your eyes (you'll have to do that after you read this material!) and imagine yourself going back in time, to perhaps age five.

In this exercise there will be two of you, but you'll both be "you." At first you will be yourself as an adult, as "Mom." Second you will be yourself as a five-year-old "Child."

Although you can clearly see each other and talk openly to each other, to everyone else you are both invisible. This means that you are free to walk around in your childhood home, with Mom and Dad (plus any other family members you choose) there. Although you can see them and talk about them, they can't see you or hear you talk.

As you begin the exercise at age five, imagine what you would have been wearing. What haircut did you have then? What did you look like? Now imagine that your adult self, Mom, is standing in front of yourself as Child. You're outside, in the grass or on the sidewalk in front of the place where you grew up. The two of you are looking at each other. The Child is thinking, "So this is what I'll look like when I grow up." And Mom is thinking, "What a cute child I was! How precious!"

Now imagine Mom sitting down in front of Child and inviting the Child to come sit on her lap. Does the Child do so? Is the Child comfortable with this level of closeness? If so, great. If not, ask the Child why. She'll tell you.

If she allows Mom to hold her, then do so for a few moments. Smell the Child's hair, perhaps dusty from play or sweet from a bath just finished. Imagine your cheek upon her hair. Feel her warmth.

In a little while, ask if she would be willing to take you on a tour of where she lives. If the answer is yes, imagine the two of you getting up and walking through the house, hand in hand. Ask the Child gentle questions as you go through the house. You will know the questions to ask.

"Could we go into the kitchen?" "Who's in the kitchen? What's she doing?" "What kind of relationship do you have with her?" "What's it like being her little girl?" "Could we go into the living room?" "Who's in the living room?" "Where's Daddy?" "What's it like being Daddy's little girl?" "Where is your room? Would you show me where you play?" "Where is it safe in your house?" "Who frightens you?"

Walk around the house with your Child for fifteen or twenty

minutes. Ask questions. Listen carefully to what she has to say. You are there in order to be positive, encouraging, loving, and gentle with her. Avoid any urges you may feel to scold her or to tell her she's done something wrong or bad. You are now there to be her close friend. If you'll listen to her and love her, she'll tell you where she hurts and why. If you're rough or mean with her, she'll do what most little girls do when threatened by a big person. She'll clam up.

After your conversation with her, go back out into the yard together again, and give her a hug. Then tell her that somehow you and she got separated when you were little. Ask her if she would be willing to be your friend. Tell her that you'll be back again to spend time with her. Give her a kiss, and say good-bye.

Step 2

The next step involves doing this exercise with your Child at every year between birth and age twenty. Spend fifteen or twenty minutes with your Child at birth, holding the child that is you, kissing her, telling her she's beautiful, counting her fingers and toes, and so on. Then pledge yourself to protect her to the best of your ability.

On the next day or a couple of days later, spend a few minutes with your Child at age one. Watch her learn to toddle. Hold her. Tell her you love her. Feel her little body in your arms.

Spend fifteen to twenty minutes with each age. At about age three or four you might begin having actual memories. Once those memories begin you might be able to converse with your Child, since memory is often tied to verbal ability. Children of this age can often communicate quite well.

There is a way of distinguishing real memories from those that you feel you may just be creating in this exercise. Real memories often have feelings associated with them. Made-up memories usually don't.

This may sound as if it's a silly exercise. It is not. One day a woman in her forties was using it. While "rummaging around in the mental attic" of her childhood house, she remembered why she spent so much time in the attic. The attic was a safe place where her father would usually not come looking for her. When she asked the Child why she needed a safe place, the Child led her to the bedroom where her father had abused her. She went to the attic to play in order to avoid being with her father, even though the attic was hot and dusty.

In another situation, a woman was going back for her Child when she discovered that she might not be right-handed, as she had supposed. Since middle childhood she had assumed she was right-handed, but her Child had led her back to an abusive situation in which her father forced her to use her left hand to stimulate him. From that moment she had denied the use of her left hand. In my office she showed me smooth writing she had recently done with her left hand, and she compared it with the choppy, scratchy writing style of her right hand.

All of these memories are in place in our memory banks. We don't usually lose them; we just repress them. Going back for the Child is a means of helping that child free herself of some negative feelings she has carried with her from childhood into adulthood.

Again, your job as Mom is to be loving, gentle, compassionate, forgiving, encouraging, positive, sweet, uplifting, nurturing, and so on. You are to be to your Child the mother that you would have wished for her to have. The objective is to help that little girl move through and beyond some of the painful experiences and memories that have haunted her—and you.

If you can't be that sort of person yet, then pick a model. June Cleaver. Timmy's mother in *Lassie*. The mother of a childhood friend. You'll probably find that the ages around which you were being abused may be particularly difficult ages for you to love your Child. That's normal. And those ages are the ones in which your Child will most need your mothering and love.

Don't scold her. Rather, tell her things such as: "He should have never done that to you. He was wrong. He was evil. You are a precious little girl. You are not at fault. I love you. I'll try to protect you against anyone who may hurt you in the future. Stay close to me. I'm strong now, and I can take care of you."

USING YOUR ANGER TO HELP YOU HEAL

Your anger can be a very productive force as you wade through this difficult process. As your anger emerges, congratulate yourself. You've probably repressed a lot of it over the years.

Just be careful that you don't use your anger to hurt yourself or your Child. Instead, use it to empower yourself. You are strong. You need not be victimized any longer. Feel the anger grow within you. If extreme anger would be helpful, let yourself go and rage; but keep the rage aimed at the person(s) who abused you. That's where it belongs.

Toward the end of this book you'll learn how your anger can enable you to help stop abuse in the lives of others. For now, however, use your anger to help you heal.

QUESTIONS FOR REFLECTION

1. What was it like to be your mother's child? How close were you two?

2. What got in the way of Mom's love and protection when you were being abused?

3. What would an ideal mother be like?

4. Is there any chance that your mom was a victim in any way (emotional, physical, sexual)?

5. In your life, how have you treated your Child? Have you been loving, kind, and encouraging? Or have you been critical, negative, and shaming?

6. Can you name one or two women who could function as your surrogate mother if you had the nerve to ask them?

═══ ACTION ITEMS ═══

1. Write a letter to your mother. If she's alive, *don't* mail it. In that letter, share with her (a) what you wish she could have been for you; (b) what happened to you in your abuse; (c) how much you wish you could have loved her.

2. Share the letter with one of the two women you named in question 6 in Questions for Reflection.

FOR SPIRITUAL GROWTH

As a month-long project, read through the book of Psalms. Write down every word mentioned that describes the character of

God. Look especially for the term *lovingkindness*, or the words *loving* and *kind* as they are used together.

Create a composite verbal picture of God using the characteristics you have found. Then apply those traits to your relationship with Him. Learn about the character of God so that you may learn to be open and trusting with Him—so that you may be healed.

Chapter 7
Profile of an Abuser

In 1987 a national news magazine featured an article dealing with men who compromise American military secrets. One paragraph was startling:

> The 58-year-old pedophile was a member of several child-sex networks, including the London-based Pedophile Information Exchange, and the Childhood Sensuality Circle in San Diego. Moreover, even a modestly thorough background check would have revealed that he had a 30-year history of molesting his two stepdaughters, his two natural daughters, and his grandchildren.[1]

A thirty-year history! Many children! Perhaps this man was an exception—someone who was extremely active in child molestation. Sadly, this conclusion is not necessarily true. According to Ann Landers, "Pedophiles averaged 238 attempted and 167 completed child molestations *each*. The *average* number of victims was 75.8 each. The *average* adolescent sexual offender may be expected to commit 380 sex crimes in his lifetime."[2] Think about it.

As this chapter progresses you may begin to see that your being victimized was probably not an isolated case in the career of someone who only abused one person and then quit. This chapter is included to help you learn about the kind of person who becomes a perpetrator.

This chapter is not provided so that you'll feel sorry for the abuser. In the end, you may find that you do feel sorry for him, for he lives with his own private hell. But feelings of pity are not at all necessary for your healing.

TYPES OF PERPETRATORS

Aggressive Versus Passive

There are different methods of classifying perpetrators. One way is to distinguish their approach to the child. Some perpetrators are aggressive; some are passive. The following diagram is provided to demonstrate the continuum from aggressive to passive abuse.

Continuum of Sexual Abuse

| Aggressive—————————————————Passive |
| (Perhaps violent)   (Nonviolent) |
| (Least common)   (Most common) |

Aggressive abusers use intimidation, threats, and/or physical strength or violence to get what they want. This man increases the level of terror. He uses fear as a weapon. He rips away the girl's hope of defending herself and leaves her emotionally stricken. He forces himself upon her, stripping away her sense of control over her life.

There are two kinds of aggressive abusers. One does not necessarily intend to hurt his victim, although he is willing to do so if necessary. He cannot tolerate anyone who resists him. If the child is cooperative, then he will usually not resort to violence. However, if the child resists him he will use threats or physical violence.

This type of abuser wants his way, and he will not tolerate defeat. He is willing to escalate to any level in order to achieve mastery. With this perpetrator, the victim has usually been chosen in advance. The abuse is not a random event.

The other type of aggressive abuser *does* intend to hurt his victim. He is of a different breed. He actually enjoys inflicting pain on his victim. He is the sadist whose sexual arousal actually pivots on the suffering and humiliation of his victim. He will tend to use more force and violence than may be necessary; he does so in order to execute his feelings of mastery over his victims.

His passions are driven by violence. To him, violence is erotic. He desires to punish the child for being a victim. He loathes the child for her weakness and wants to destroy her because she's so weak. Actually, it is himself that he loathes and wishes to destroy. But he is acting out this message on a helpless person.

The sadist's core is composed of self-hatred. Hurting his victim becomes an almost ritualistic purging of his own inadequacies. The child symbolizes qualities that he hates in himself: a sense of weakness, of being out of control, of humiliation. The child he abuses becomes the object of his punishment, which is unconsciously aimed at himself.

The greater the level of his victim's fear, distress, and pain, the more significant and erotic the experience is to him. His sexual gratification is tied to his victim's terrors. This abuser is more likely to choose a stranger to abuse. Obviously, it's difficult to have an ongoing relationship with someone whom one is beating and raping (although even this type of relationship does occur). More often, the victim is seen as being disposable, expendable—a thing that exists to be used as a means toward a distorted emotional end.

Whether the sadistic abuser uses a stranger or a child he knows, it is likely that he has played out the scene in his mind several times before the abuse. Although the victim may not have been selected yet, there is usually an element of premeditation involved.

Many sadists find excitement in torturing animals. They frequently have fantasies of strength and power, with sexual overtones. Therefore, when they select a child for abuse, they frequently have all of the details worked out—location, time, type of activity, and so on.

Of those men who choose to use children for their sexual gratification, the sadist is the most damaging. However, recovery from all forms of sexual abuse is usually very difficult. All sexual abuse is destructive.

Furthermore, each victim has her own personality strength, her own ability to process horrible events in her life. Each woman faces her own personal hell in her own way, with her own strengths and level of support.

Passive abusers use warmth, charm, personal need, manipulation, and relationship to obtain sexual favors. Dealing with passive abusers requires a change of dynamics from dealing with aggressive abusers. Passive abusers appear warm and genuine; yet they use that very warmth to hurt and manipulate. Love becomes a mixed message. Warmth becomes suspect. Genuineness becomes confusing.

Passive abusers rely upon the child's trust, then use that trust to commit their destructive acts. It is as if they offer candy and then give poison. They offer a warm hug and say gentle things, and then rip the child's self-esteem. Deceit and distortion are their stock-in-trade.

Children are usually taught to trust adults and therefore are vulnerable in the presence of adults. Most adults have the child's best interests at heart. But some adults use this trust to invade and plunder.

The passive abuser is most often a relative or a friend of the family. He is usually a trusted adult. He does not need to use force to get what he wants because he is able to contrive situations in which he can use the relationship to get what he wants. If he is not a direct family member, frequently he has worked at ingratiating himself with the child's parents, seeming to be a safe friend.

He often attempts to make the sexual encounter appear to be a game. Or he may try to convince the child that he has "special" needs. If the child loves him, she will help him meet those needs. He may tell the child that he's helping her get ready for normal adult sexuality. He may say that what's going on is normal for all people.

He relies upon the child's wish not to displease him, even though to the victim his request may seem unpleasant or even horribly distasteful. If he feels it is necessary, he may tell the girl that she *has* to do sexual acts with him and that she has no choice in the matter. If the abuser is a family member, he may threaten to break apart the family if she doesn't cooperate. One victim was forced into sex with an uncle because the uncle held a rifle to the head of her infant sister, threatening to kill the baby. Her aunt begged her not to make her uncle kill the baby.

In dealing with the passive abuser, a victim's emotional difficulty is the double-bind message inherent within the abuse. This message confuses love with horror, intimacy with manipulation, closeness with shame, and so on. For this reason many adult victims report situations in which they are badly treated by spouses, employers, or friends. Yet they defend the other person's right to harm them. The pattern is established during childhood and is often tied to sexual abuse.

It is not unusual for victims to mature into adulthood carrying a deep internal struggle with how to reconcile positive feelings of emotional closeness with fears of emotional pain when close to another person. Victims frequently find themselves confused, struggling to separate desires for emotional closeness from fears surrounding sexuality. Some avoid sexuality to lower the emotional stress of this double bind.

The passive abuser often stalks the victim for some time, watching, fantasizing, and plotting before making his move. He is usually quite sure that the child will not tell anyone. To be sure that the child does not tell, after the abuse he frequently adds a "closer" of some sort: "This is our secret. Nobody must ever know." "If you love me you'll never tell anyone." "If you ever say anything about this I'll say you're lying—and who do you think they'll believe, you or me?" "You were responsible for this. You made me do it to you." "If you tell anyone I'll kill myself." "If you tell anyone I'll kill your kitten (or your sister, your mother, and so on)." Like the aggressive abuser, the passive abuser damages the victim's self-esteem.

Incest Versus Molestation

Another way of categorizing abusers involves the type of relationship the abuser has with the victim. Some persons abuse relatives. This type of abuse is called *incest*. Others abuse strangers. This is called *molestation*. And in between there is a gray area in which close family friends, teachers, clergy, and others may fall.

Generally speaking, the closer the relationship of the abuser with the victim, the more difficult it will be for the victim to sort out her feelings and relationships in later years.

Male Versus Female Abusers

Most abusers are male. Some are female, including mothers, baby-sitters, and relatives. Some fondle their children whether the infant is male or female. Some men and a few women actively seduce young boys.

STATISTICS OF FREQUENCY

Various studies tell us that girls growing up in this country have a very high chance of being sexually abused. Sanford (1980) estimates that in America today, there is a one-in-four chance that a little girl will be the victim of incest, child molestation, or rape by the time she is eighteen years old. Moore and Riekens (1985) state that research conducted on the nation's university campuses indicates that 19.2 percent of all girls and 8.6 percent of all boys have been victimized (sexually abused) in the United States. Bass and Davis (1988) say that one out of three girls and one out of seven boys are sexually abused by the time they reach age eighteen.

One-in-five; one-in-four; one-in-three—the point is obvious. Sexual abuse is not an isolated problem occurring infrequently in dark corners. You have many sisters.

WHO ARE THE ABUSERS?

Who are the abusers, and what do we know about them? Sources of information vary in their observations. Following are a few relevant published statements.

1. Men are usually the abusers. Sanford estimates that 97 percent of child sexual abuse is committed by males.

2. The majority of victims are female, but studies vary in this regard. Sanford says that 60 percent to 90 percent of victims are female, while Moore and Riekens estimate closer to a two-to-one ratio, female-to-male victims.

3. Moore and Riekens believe that 90 percent of all reported

cases of abuse are committed by someone the child knows and trusts, and 27 percent are from the child's immediate household.

4. Although sexual abuse can occur at any age, the age of highest frequency of abuse is eleven (Moore and Riekens).

5. Sanford estimates that abusers usually begin their molesting activities before their fortieth birthday, and 80 percent had committed their first offense by age thirty. Their activity frequently begins in adolescence.

6. Sanford states that the average molester of female children will choose sixty-two to sixty-four victims in his career, but this statistic is probably low. (Ann Landers, cited early in this chapter, indicates the number may be as high as 167 victims.)

7. Larry Corrigan indicates that the average incestuous father commits over one hundred abusive acts before being charged.[3]

PERSONALITY PROFILE OF AN ABUSER

It may be helpful to look at some personality traits common among abusers. An important observation is that many theorists do not believe that sex is the primary motivation for sexual abuse. Often the perpetrator has other needs for which sex is a substitute. These may include needs for power, intimacy, playfulness, and holding or being held.

When the molestation turns violent, other needs are generally being addressed. The abuser may feel a need for power or dominance; may associate erotic acts with a need for hostility or aggression; may feel that his life is out of control and attempts to manage it by violence. To the perpetrator, sex is usually symbolic of something else.

Furthermore, in virtually all cases of abuse, the perpetrator has a strong sense of personal worthlessness. He almost always suffers from critically low self-esteem. Regardless of how he may appear to the child he is abusing, when seen from the eyes of another adult, the abuser is usually somewhat socially isolated or backward.

WHY DO PERPETRATORS CHOOSE CHILDREN?

The first reason a perpetrator chooses children is emotional immaturity. He is erotically stimulated by children. He has not grown up—he is stuck in some serious ways. He may not appear to be emotionally immature, but he is.

Dealing with his own inadequacies, he is less comfortable with adult sexuality than he is with child sexuality. He probably does not feel capable of achieving his ends through normal adult means. In his own psychological world he is immature and associates children with sexual arousal. He feels more in control if the other person in the relationship is a child.

He has likely been physically or sexually abused himself. There is a high correlation between people who abuse and those who have been victims.

PERPETRATING AGAINST CHILDREN IS EVIL

The perpetrator is also dealing with evil in his life. There is a more or less universal taboo against adults sexually molesting children. In point of fact, the taboo may be more true of *talking about* abuse than of *committing* abuse. Many assume that in Western culture the taboo against sexual abuse unquestionably exists, based on Judeo-Christian principles. Members of our churches and synagogues uphold the taboo, and it is codified into our legal system.

Yet in reality a patriarchal system dominates many families. Males often have inordinate control over the rest of the family. Molesters usually know this and play upon it. Consequently, often there is a wide gap between what we as a culture say we believe about sexual abuse and what we do actually believe.

Most people believe that adults who molest children are committing wrong acts. They may be considered evil. It is reasonable to call the abuser a deviant person, since he is deviating from stated religious and social norms.

Yet there also appears to be a cultural taboo regarding talking about sexual abuse. It remains a hidden thing, often kept "in the closet" for generations. In many cases the perpetrator is acting out multigenerational behavior. He is not all that rare. Many families have a molester living in their midst or hiding in their closet.

Hence, there remains a tension between what we as a culture say we believe, and what we do about our stated belief system. This fact often wreaks havoc upon a woman's ability to heal.

Personal Selfishness of the Abuser

The perpetrator is a self-oriented person. No matter what he may tell his victim about helping her "understand" sexuality, he is focused only upon himself. He has no knowledge of or concern for the damage he is doing. Everything he does is motivated by pure self-interest. At the least, most people would call him completely irresponsible.

WHY YOU NEED TO KNOW ABOUT
YOUR ABUSER

Why is it important for you to know that your abuser was personally inadequate, immature, acting wrongfully, deviant, selfish, and irresponsible? There are two reasons. First, many victims do not know or believe that the person who abused them was psychologically immature and inadequate. *All* abusers are deviant, even those who seem committed to spirituality and the church.

The second reason may be even more important. Many victims still believe that *they* were wrong, possibly even responsible for their own abuse. They believe that somehow they enticed it or deserved it. Some victims even defend the perpetrator's right to abuse them.

Therefore, understand that an abuser's acts are indefensible. Regardless of the feelings you may yet harbor about him, he was evil and selfish. If you feel he was right in what he did, then your perspective needs adjustment. If you are angry with him—so angry that you could spit bullets—then you're on track. It's OK to be angry. You were subjected to a criminal act.

Victims often struggle with the association between intimacy and shame. Even as adults, their feelings of emotional closeness with loved ones often lead to feelings of shame, guilt, and self-loathing. Many victims attempt to resolve this problem by staying away from close friendships of almost any kind. Others act out an unconscious message that says they're good only for sex. They become promiscuous.

Why would a girl feel self-loathing and shame as a result of an experience that she did not initiate or desire? Understanding the answer is important. As you think about the person who abused you, ask yourself, *Why do I feel shamed and guilty? Why do I have such low self-esteem? Why do I continue to allow what he did to control my life?*

ADDITIONAL FACTS ABOUT PERPETRATORS

There are a few other characteristics of abusers that you need to know.

1. Perpetrators usually try to blame their victims for the abuse.

2. Passive abusers frequently say that their victims were acting seductively toward them. They "just couldn't help themselves" and were "seduced."

3. Aggressive abusers frequently speak of their victims' helplessness—as if this was sufficient reason for their abuse.

4. Abusers in general attempt to cast blame upon their own mothers or wives for "not meeting my needs." Blame is a primary tool of the abuser. It's never their fault—always someone else's.

5. Women who have been abused often marry abusers or abuse victims. Or they marry men who are so emotionally dead that they never talk about it.

6. If the abuse occurs between brother and sister, the brother is frequently acting out feelings of being intimidated by his peers. He turns to his sister, usually younger, to fill his needs for affection and power.

7. If a brother is abusing a sister and there are other brothers in a family, often word gets out and the other brothers join in.

8. If a brother is abusing a sister, there is likely a family history of other sexual abuse.

9. Mothers who have been abused within their own families of origin frequently deny the reality of their daughters' abuse.

10. If a girl is being abused and she is unable to find help from her family, *something is dramatically wrong within her family system.*

SUMMARY

What kind of profile does one find in a man who would sexually abuse a girl? First, he's probably socially immature and does not have a normal, healthy range of successful adult relationships. Second, his sexual acts with the child are not primarily sexually motivated. They are geared toward meeting needs in his own life.

Third, he's probably dealing with severely low self-esteem. He attempts to demonstrate his power by using children. Fourth, he's a person of low moral integrity. This is often confusing to victims, since many perpetrators outwardly appear to be deeply religious. But their religion is patently false.

Fifth, he has probably worked toward convincing his victim that she's responsible for what he did to her. In any case, he likely has not accepted responsibility for his actions. He may have conned others into seeing the situation through his eyes. Perpetrators are often great manipulators. They are good at getting others to agree with them, even when they are lying.

Sixth, his victim is probably not the only girl he has abused. There are likely many others. Finally, the sicker he is, the more likely it is that he uses some sort of violence or torture in his abuse.

Now pause and reflect for a moment. Even if this person appeared to be the nicest person in the world, is he really a nice person? Use your rational, cognitive, thinking ability for a moment. Do you need to defend him? Is it reasonable that you should feel guilty and dirty because of what he did to you? Should you accept feeling stained and humiliated because he acted out his misjudgments on your body?

Is it reasonable to continue to think that you may have somehow brought the abuse upon yourself? Can you stop thinking that somehow you deserved what happened to you? This man was a perpetrator. He was a sexual abuser. Can you at least rationally accept the fact that he, not you, was at fault?

As you process these questions, give yourself permission to say no to him, at least in your mind. Give yourself permission to say no to those covert messages that still tell you that you were responsible.

QUESTIONS FOR REFLECTION

1. Reflect upon your abuse. Was it passive or aggressive? Or were there aspects of both?

2. How would you describe the emotional maturity and spiritual character of your abuser?

3. Reflect upon the way you felt about yourself following abuse. Are you able to connect with any of those feelings now? How did your perpetrator make you feel? Is it reasonable for you to carry those feelings into the rest of your life?

4. Reflect upon what an abused rag doll might be feeling. Are any of her feelings yours?

5. Use any four words to describe your abuser:

a. _____   b. _____

c. _____   d. _____

═══ ACTION ITEMS ═══

1. Write down feelings you had both during and after being abused. Be thorough. What did you feel *then*? What do you feel *now*? (Use two columns, *then* and *now*.)

2. Purchase a rag doll. Using whatever you may have on hand at home, alter the doll to reflect how your abuser made you feel about yourself. (Color, rip, tear, paint, and so on.) This exercise is intended to help you connect with a very badly broken *you*. If you become frightened, overwhelmed, or so angry that you feel you're losing control, stop for a while. Take a breather. Get help if you need it.

3. After you're finished, look at the doll for a while through the eyes of someone who loves her. That someone will eventually be you. What would it mean for you to love her? What does she need from you? Write down some of these thoughts.

4. In your own handwriting, copy the following statement to the person(s) who abused you:

What you did to me was wrong. I don't care what kind of pain you might have had in your own life. I don't care what kind of needs you might have had or felt you had. What you did to me was wrong.

I will allow myself to be angry with you! I may choose someday to forgive you—perhaps, perhaps not. But today I am angry with you!

You made me feel guilty and dirty. But I am not dirty and guilty. As I stand before God, I am not dirty and guilty. I refuse to accept that feeling of filth and guilt any longer.

Those are your *burdens, not mine, to carry. Carry them!* You *are responsible for what you did.* You *are the person who is guilty and dirty.*

Now, continue with some of your own thoughts. Write as much as you wish. End the statement in a personal way.

5. Write a statement about some of the differences between sexuality and being emotionally close to a person.

6. Write about the type of person your ideal mother would be if she existed. Write what she would have said to your abuser; how she would have wrapped her arms around you and cried; how she would have nourished and cared for you; and how she would have protected you.

7. Imagine yourself through the eyes of this mother. Close your eyes and feel her wrapping her arms around you. Allow yourself to cry in her arms if you wish. Hear her telling you she loves you. Feel her support. Hear her telling you that you're not guilty or dirty. Allow her love to wash over you.

FOR SPIRITUAL GROWTH

1. Read Psalm 37:1–7. What does this passage say about evil people? What does it tell you to do about your past, present, and future?

2. Read Psalm 91:1–16, and reflect upon how you may learn to connect with a God who wishes to love and protect you. Is it God's fault that you were abused? Should He have protected you? Since He allows evil to exist in the world, how can He still love you in a way that you can identify, feel, and accept?

3. Read Isaiah 50:7–9, and reflect upon a scene in which your abuser stands before God and accuses you. Muse about what God's response might be. Picture yourself standing next to God, and listen to your abuser attempting to blame you for all that he did to you.

4. Spend five minutes in prayer. Ask God to give you the strength to wade through all that is ahead of you so that you can become free from the chains of your abuse.

Chapter 8
The Family System of Abuse

Abuse in the family affects all *its members, although this is not always readily acknowledged.*[1]

In this chapter we'll look at the family system of the abused child. Primarily we'll view the type of home in which a girl is abused more than once, usually over a long period of time. However, much of the chapter will apply to the family systems of all abuse victims.

If you are an incest victim (abused by anyone within the extended family), this chapter is especially for you. However, even if you were abused by a nonfamily member—if you were unable *for any reason* to bring your abuse to the attention of your parents—this chapter is for you too.

Many parents of sexually abused children simply do not know that the abuse occurred. There is ample room for parental naiveté and genuine ignorance. When such parents discover that their child is an abuse victim, they are shocked. They don't know how to react or how to help their child.

On the other hand, repetitive abuse—especially incest—rarely occurs without the collusion of the entire family. Someone *must* have known and chose to ignore the situation. At the very least in this scenario, the perpetrator was so skilled in setting up the situation that he was able to shield other family members from knowledge of the abuse. In long-term repetitive abuse, this possibility is highly unlikely. Naturally, this situation is difficult for many women to accept.

How could it be true that in a family in which something as awful as sexual abuse is happening, nobody seems to notice the victim's symptoms? Nobody steps in to say, "Tell me what's going on here." Nobody takes the initiative to stop the pain. Nobody seems even to notice that there is pain. Nobody hears the victim's silent screams. Nobody seems to notice anything. Why doesn't the victim feel she can turn to others for help?

If Mother is dead and Father is the perpetrator, then the answer may be obvious. But most abusive systems don't fit that description.

The answer to repetitive, long-term, or frequent abuse is that the family itself is dysfunctional—unhealthy. The family either provides the emotional/relational soil within which sexual abuse can flourish, or it is unable to effectively react to the pathology once it becomes known.

If you are such a victim, something about your family was dysfunctional. Regardless of the veneer of family life that other people saw, under the surface something was not functioning properly. A virus was loose, and either nobody was willing to recognize the symptoms or nobody was willing to risk confronting and defeating it.

Long-term sexual abuse in a family has the tacit, not overt, support of family members. In all likelihood the family doesn't sit around the kitchen table one evening and say, "Let's have Dad rape Susie tonight, and let's do nothing to stop it and then never talk about it." More likely, the family system's nature allows the abuse to happen, then is not equipped to stop it or to help heal the victim.

THE EXTENT OF INTRAFAMILIAL ABUSE IS UNKNOWN

There probably are no truly accurate figures reflecting the amount of sexual abuse within families. Such a figure would be difficult to obtain. The reason is that *families tend to cover up*.

Families tend not to speak openly about family problems. This is even more true of "sick" families than of families in general. Sick families often guard family secrets even more fiercely than do healthy ones. Since sexual abuse is sick behavior, it is likely that even the most professional and scientific research on families will uncover less abuse than exists.

Moore and Riekens indicate that "Ninety percent of all *reported* sexual abuse cases are committed by someone the child knows and trusts; 27 percent are from the child's immediate household—the father or stepfather."[2] Even within that statement are important variables. Does the word "household" include brothers, stepbrothers, grandparents, and other live-in family members? Use of the word *reported* implies that many incidents are not reported. Since sick families try to keep their secrets firmly hidden, the majority of family abuse is probably not reported.

REASONS WHY SOME FAMILIES DON'T STOP THE ABUSE

Even families that appear to be normal and healthy often cover up or ignore sexual abuse. Following are some of the reasons why.

Fear of Punishment

Mother may be afraid to say anything because she'll be beaten up. Or she may fear that if she tells the police, her husband will be dragged off to jail. Then the family's income will be lost; they will be destitute; and perhaps the children will be moved to foster homes.

Victims frequently have the same fears, so they too will keep their abuse a secret. Victims may have other concerns as well. Perhaps Mother will reject her daughter if she finds out that some family member has been fondling or having intercourse with the girl. Many victims also fear that somehow they are responsible for what happened. Other victims fear being held responsible for the destruction of their parents' marriage if Mother finds out that Dad has been sexually active with their daughter.

Healthy family systems talk together about even the darkest pain and fear. It is the family system already in trouble that creates a climate in which a girl cannot share openly with her parents.

Fear of Social Stigma

Imagine growing up hearing the neighbors whispering, "Her father rapes her three times a week" or "Her brother fondles her" or "She's in bed with her granddad." Sexual abuse is so ugly that nobody feels comfortable talking about what's going on in the family. This statement applies equally to perpetrator and victim; offending adult and nonoffending adult; child and sibling; guilty and innocent.

Healthy families have the strength to deal even with the terribly uncomfortable nature of abuse; to get it out in the open; to support and love the victim. Sick families usually don't have that strength.

Homeostasis of the Family System

Families are organisms, just as are amoebas, human beings, corporations, churches, and nations. Organisms tend to seek *homeostasis*. That is, organisms like to feel balanced, in control, internally stable, at peace, with a comfortable sense of equilibrium. To obtain homeostasis, sick family systems are often willing to sacrifice one or more members. They're willing to allow an adult male to rape a female child, "if that's what it takes to keep things calm around here."

In this kind of system, if a victim actually seeks help—if someone "squeals" to an authority who effects change—then the established homeostasis is disrupted. This may sound crazy, but it is true.

In some dysfunctional family configurations, there is a role called the scapegoat. This individual is assigned all the sickness, pain, and pathology of the whole family system. In some cases it appears to the family system that one family member must be sacrificed in order for the rest of the family to survive. When this occurs, it is the scapegoat who is usually given up. Many victims are their family systems' scapegoats.

Dysfunctional family systems often exist for generations with a distorted sense of equilibrium, seeking a pained and pathological homeostasis—even though this balance is grossly immoral, illegal, and totally unacceptable. Sexual abuse within a family system unquestionably qualifies a family for the title of *dysfunctional*.

Organisms seek homeostasis. Sick families often would rather keep the sickness than face making real changes. Sexual abuse is often an intergenerational family condition.

Inadequacy of Family Members

Where there is a perpetrator, there are often other family members who are equally vulnerable in some way. Often it is not only the victim who risks the loss of love by telling of the abuse. Within the abusive system there are frequently other nonoffending family members, none of whom take direct, serious, effective action to terminate the abuse. Usually these family members are somehow disempowered. They don't have the courage or the power to do anything about the abuse.

Again, *something is wrong* with a family system that allows ongoing abuse. *Something is wrong* with brothers and sisters, mothers, uncles or aunts, grandparents, and others who, especially over a period of years, must know that something is wrong with Sally, yet do nothing about it. Perhaps Father projects a deeply devout and religious image that nobody would wish to tarnish. Or he may be too physically brutal for anyone to risk challenging him. Mother may be too emotionally fragile for anyone to risk letting her in on the "awful secret." Brother may be in on the abuse. Or, conversely, he may protect himself against any direct emotional involvement in order to shield himself from knowledge of the abuse.

The point is that in long-term abuse and incest, often others besides the abuser and victim know what's going on. Or at least others know that *something* is going on. But for some reason the nonoffending members don't step in and take protective action.

The family system may be weak, inadequate, ineffective, fearful, out of control, or badly balanced.

SOME SIGNALS OF SEXUAL ABUSE

When human beings are deeply traumatized, there are frequently signals indicating an internal struggle. When children act substantially different from how they or their peers normally act or react, families should pay attention. Children often don't have the adult, intellectual, cognitive skills to express themselves. But when they are hurting their behavior usually changes.

Let's look at some of the symptoms or behaviors often closely associated with sexual abuse.

1. Seventy-five to one hundred percent of all prostitutes indicate sexual abuse in their background (Moore and Riekens, 1985).

2. Seventy-five percent of all drug and alcohol abusers indicate that they have been sexual abuse victims (Moore and Riekens). Substance abuse in general is often characteristic of older children who have been abused (Herman and Hirschman, 1981; Riggs, 1982; Spencer, 1978; Summit, 1983; Vander, Mey, and Neff, 1982).

3. Hostile-aggressive behavior is a frequent signal of sexual abuse (Tucker, 1981; Bess and Janssen, 1982; De Francis, 1970; Tufts, 1984).

4. Some children retreat to less than normally assertive behavior (Shaw and Meier, 1983). See number 3; either way, there is a change in normal patterns of behavior.

5. Antisocial behavior is a frequent symptom (De Francis, 1970).

6. Delinquency frequently occurs with school-age children (Blumberg, 1978; De Francis, 1970; Meiselman, 1979; Vander, Mey, and Neff, 1982).

7. Stealing sometimes becomes a pattern with older children (Weiss and others, 1985).

8. Tantrums may recur (Adams and Tucker, 1981).

9. Some studies have noted a tendency for some sexually abused children to exhibit withdrawal behavior (Adams and Tucker, 1981; Burgess and Holmstrom, 1975; Jiles, 1981; Riggs, 1982). Such withdrawal often takes the forms of:

- Living in a fantasy world (Riggs, 1982).
- Staying inside the home and refusing to leave (Burgess and Holmstrom, 1975).
- Regressive behaviors, such as a return to thumb sucking, fear of the dark, or fear of strangers (Adams and Tucker, 1982; Brassard and others, 1983; DHHS, 1981; Herman and Hirschman, 1981; James, 1977; Riggs, 1982; Spencer, 1978; Weiss and others, 1985).
- Bed-wetting.
- Sexual acting out with other children or even with adults.

These are just a few of the very obvious, easily observable, and documented symptoms exhibited by children who have been abused. Wouldn't you think that any parent who is even remotely involved with his or her child would tune in to these and perhaps many other symptoms, begin to ask questions, and seek help? As an adult, wouldn't you take action and attempt to meet the needs of the child? Wouldn't you give this matter top priority until the situation was properly remedied, the symptoms ceased, and the child was back to her old self again?

HOW FAMILIES CONTROL THEIR VICTIMS

There are three main ways that sick families control abused children and keep them victimized.

Isolation

Sexually abusive families are usually fairly adept at keeping victims away from help. Sometimes these family systems create an atmosphere in which any outsider is suspect. Individuals who might take active steps to remedy the situation are often particularly suspect. Such persons include teachers, therapists, clergy members, coaches, physicians, social workers, police officers, and attorneys.

The abusive family system keeps most extrafamilial relationships at a superficial level. Close relationships with persons other than family members are frequently avoided by both the family and the victim. Obviously, perpetrators don't want outsiders observing the family system, figuring things out, and blowing the whistle. As for the victim, even if she would love to have a close girlfriend, she may be afraid that such a friend would find out her secret, tell others, and cause further rejection. Therefore, victims frequently aid and abet their own isolation.

Threats

There are many threats that keep victims silent. Some examples follow.

- If you tell anyone, I'll make you wish you were never born.
- If you tell anyone, I'll kill you (or your mother, your sister, your puppy).
- If you tell anyone, I'll tell them stories about you. You'll lose all your friends.
- If you tell anyone, you'll be responsible for breaking apart our family. It will be your fault.
- If you tell anyone, we'll kick you out of the family.

There is always the threat of losing what the victim needs perhaps more than anything else in the world: the love and support of her family. Even if the family is sick and painful, it's all that many victims have. Unfair as it may be, dysfunctional as it may sound, many victims stay in abusive families because they believe that they cannot find love outside the family. To risk losing what little love one may have can be a risk too great to take. Consequently, many victims endure the abuse until they are old enough to successfully flee. Then they leave, but they don't blow the whistle on the way out.

Inversion of Good and Bad

A third method used by abusing families is the inversion of good and bad. In this approach, good is cast in a bad light, and bad becomes good. Obviously, this skewing of the child's compass becomes terribly confusing, and it often remains with the victim for decades.

Children have an internal sense of right and wrong. They may not be thoroughly versed in morals, but they sense or know that the perpetrator's touching them feels wrong.

Therefore, the perpetrator must somehow cause the child to believe that she is wrong, and he is right. This is often not too difficult, since children are usually taught that adults are right and have children's best interests at heart. Following are some statements of perpetrators used to accomplish this task.

- I'm going to teach you something that you'll have to know when you're a big girl. All big girls need to know about this.
- What we're doing is not wrong. It's normal.
- You are a dirty little tramp, and I'm going to teach you about sex.
- This will be fun, and we'll make it our secret.
- If you want me to love you, then this is part of what love is all about.
- I need you so much. If you love me, you'll . . .

What were you told? What game, or secret, or threat was used on you? There almost had to be something. Can you identify it?

The inversion of right and wrong often causes a deep level of questioning to occur within the victim. Her values, perceptions, and feelings all come into question. Worse, she learns to question her own internal compass. This questioning often leads to a life-style in which the victim questions her own right to have any feelings, perceptions, or values. Having had to reach so deeply into herself to justify her abuser's perspective, she often ends up changing the settings of her internal compass. What used to read *north* now reads *south*. What used to read *bad* now reads *good*. What used to read *right* now reads *wrong*.

Once you understand this, you can readily see why sexual abuse victims often feel disoriented. One victim asked if she was crazy because she frequently found herself wondering where she was. Another victim told of relating to people in ways that were almost totally inappropriate—laughing at things that nobody else found funny, misinterpreting sentences spoken by others, and so on. Yet another victim reported waking in the middle of the night and trying to remember who she was.

If a perpetrator can convince a victim that it is right for him to use her, then he has created an endless availability for what he wants. As we have noted, this task is not as difficult as it may appear. Proof of this fact lies in the perception of most victims: many carry strong feelings that *they* were at fault for the abuse!

THE ROLE OF MOTHER

In abusive family systems, Mother plays a key role. Often victims find it hard to know how active a role their mother had in their pain. To be fair, Mother is often a victim herself. If so, she may be clinically unaware of what is going on in her children's lives. As a victim, Mother may tend to block conscious awareness of what is happening to her daughter. The perpetrator often sets her up too, to be out of the way so he has access to the kids.

Women who were molested often fall for molesters, sometimes even marrying them, just like girls with blond dads often fall for blond boyfriends. Coming from a family system of abuse, they have learned to speak the language of denial, dissociation, and codependency. They often marry men who appear to be good but who later reveal themselves to be molesters.

As the scenario unfolds, however, it becomes more apparent that Mother played a significant role—even as a nonplayer. Mother may not have been a perpetrator; she did not have to be one in order to have been a coconspirator. She did not even have to be conscious of her role to have played an active part in her daughter's suffering. The fact that Mother didn't know about or didn't step in and protect her abused child *is significant*. Following are several reasons why Mother may not have done anything.

Abused Mother

As startling as it may sound, many mothers of sexual abuse victims are themselves sexual abuse victims. One would think that, having been abused herself, such a mother would leap at the throat of anyone abusing her daughter. And some do. However, unless Mom has grown past denial about her own abuse, and unless she has done her own necessary healing, she will be more psychologically prone to deny the reality of her daughter's abuse. Indeed, she may not even see the abuse, even when it happens before her very eyes. Denial is immensely powerful.

Weak Mother

Sometimes Mother is weak. The weakness may be physical, as in having cancer and fighting for her life. She may be so weakened by chronic physical ailments that all she can do is to take care of herself.

On the other hand, Mother may be physically healthy but emotionally fragile and weak. She may not feel she has the strength to confront the abuser. In this scenario the daughter sometimes takes on Mom's household chores, including sexually servicing Dad.

Helpless Mother

Mother may be physically strong but mentally weak. She might even have sought help but received inadequate or incorrect advice from a counselor. It wasn't many years ago (1963, to be exact) that it was a criminal offense for professionals to intervene in the domain of the family.

Mother may have been so dominated by her husband that she became timid and mouselike. Even though she may have suspected something was wrong, she did not have the relational power or the personal fortitude to do anything about it. She may have wished or prayed that the abuse would stop, but she may not have had the strength or the courage to take action herself.

This helplessness can become a chronic disability. A condition called _learned helplessness_ applies in this case. A mother may be so intimidated and beaten down by her husband that even though she knows her daughter is being abused, she may simply not believe that there is any way out of the situation.

A classic study was made of this syndrome several years ago. Researchers put a dog into a cage. The cage was divided into two halves by a short plywood wall. The dog could easily leap over the wall. The researchers placed an electric grid on each side of the cage, enabling them to electrify the floor on either side.

First they would shock the dog on one side of the cage, and the dog would leap over the barrier to safety.

Then they would shock the dog on the second side of the cage, and the dog would leap back to the first side.

Then the researchers electrified both sides of the cage and made it impossible for the dog to escape the pain. At first the dog leaped about wildly, attempting to escape the pain by hopping from side to side and clawing at the cage walls. Eventually, though, the dog stopped leaping and simply lay down in a corner of the cage. No matter how high the researchers boosted the electrical shock, the dog made no further attempt at escape. The animal had learned that he was helpless—that no matter what he did, escape was impossible. Victims often learn this. Some moms do too.

That is learned helplessness. That is why some mothers don't even try to help their daughters. That is also why some daughters don't believe they have any realistic hope of escaping their abuse. Some victims just continue to take the abuse until they grow up and can move out of the house.

Emotionally Unavailable Mother

Another kind of mother who does not rescue her daughter is emotionally absent. Her unavailability may have many different sources. One victim reported that her mother had been abused by her father (the victim's grandfather). When the victim's grandfather and father abused her, Mother had emotionally "checked out" and did not intervene.

Mother may be too emotionally fragile to handle the ugliness and pain of an abusive situation. The child knows this and will frequently try to protect Mother from the painful knowledge.

Emotionally Cool Mother

Mother may be so cool and aloof from the daughter or from the whole family that the victim feels that Mom may not even care. Even worse, the victim may feel that if she shares the abuse with her mother, Mom may retreat even further away emotionally.

Tyrant Mother

If Mother is seen as a tyrant, then the victim is faced with a hard dilemma. How would one go about sharing painful and humiliating information with a tyrant? Doubtless she already knows that the response will not be the sensitivity, gentleness, openness, and caring that she needs.

Exhausted Mother

Mother may be overworked and undersupported. She may have six other children to care for, as well as an alcoholic husband and a dying mother. She may not have the time or energy to care.

Deceased Mother

Mother may have died. The child may be living with a step-mother or with only one parent.

Mother's Own Emotional Problems

Many women who marry perpetrators have their own emotional problems. These problems frequently become barriers between mother and child, thereby inhibiting a victim from coming to Mother for help.

Mother's Own Sexual Dysfunction

Some mothers have big problems with their own sexuality, and they convey this attitude in everything they do or say. It is not unusual for victims' mothers to be sexually cold toward their husbands. One woman's mother let herself go physically, became grossly fat, and slept in a separate bedroom. Another victim's mother was sharply critical of anything to do with sex or sexuality. She often belittled her husband and called his sexual drive a weakness. She too slept in a separate bedroom. Yet another victim's mother was a Victorian, prudish woman who adopted the belief that sex was for procreation only. To her any other use of sex was unspiritual.

Some perpetrators actually set the mother up to be separate and isolated because they are really stimulated by girls. This type of abuser may say he was justified in what he did because he "kept it in the family" and did not have affairs. So some mothers appear to be or become dysfunctional owing to the success of the perpetrator's well-laid plans.

Frequently the mother of a victim is in some way attempting to repress her own sexuality. Some theorists speculate that because of her discomfort with her own sexuality, such a mother may in some way offer up her daughter to the father as a substitute for her own sexual involvement, or at least as a peace offering. MacFarlane and others offer the following thought:

> Because of her passive-dependent stance, the mother may not move to protect the child and may side with the father if the incest is disclosed, for fear of losing his support and protection. Some even feel that the mother may consciously or unconsciously "set up" the incest in order to free herself from her husband's sexual demands.[3]

Broadhurst takes the theory further, indicating that mothers who didn't know the abuse was taking place or who knew but did nothing to stop or report it should be charged with child endangerment.[4] Moore and Riekens state, "The law takes the position the mother knows what has been going on, or if she doesn't, *she should!*"[5]

It becomes apparent, then, that mothers play a substantial role in the lives of victims. This role can be played actively, as in cases of maternal sexual abuse, or passively, as when mother turns a deaf ear or is unavailable for help. Either way, hurt results. Few girls are sexually abused within a family system without wishing they could turn to their mother for help and hoping that their mother will save them. When Mother does not, the victim experiences additional damage.

Some Effects of Mother's Unavailability

When God created family systems He planned them to be run by a tandem team: mother and father. If part of that system fails and the adult male begins damaging a child, the other half of the team should be there to challenge the abuser and protect the child. If this does not occur, then in the child's mind there must be a reason. Following are the options a child has in evaluating the situation.

1. Mother doesn't know. *Hidden messages*: (a) The way to handle difficult problems is to ignore them and hope they'll go away. (b) Denial is an effective method of anxiety or problem management.

2. Mother knows, but is powerless to help me. *Hidden messages*: (a) Women are helpless when in the presence of perpetrators (or possibly in the presence of men in general). (b) Resisting is hopeless (learned helplessness). (c) Women should just learn to submit and bear life even when being treated badly.

3. Mother knows, but hates me. *Hidden messages*: (a) I am unlovable and/or responsible for the abuse. (b) I am being punished for being bad. (c) Women cannot be trusted or relied upon in time of need. (d) Close relationships with women should be avoided, since women won't help you even when you're hurting. (e) Women are the enemy—competitors to be beaten, especially when fighting for male attention and affection.

THE PERPETRATOR AS FAMILY MEMBER

Chapter 7 deals with the profile of an abuser, but in this section we'll focus upon some of the distinctive dynamics of the family system within which a family member is the perpetrator.

Some theorists believe that the sexually abusive male family member is a domineering, authoritarian type of person, at least within the family system. He may not be powerful outside the family, but he certainly exerts his sense of power and control within the family structure. MacFarlane and others say:

Most of the older studies have looked at preadolescent or adolescent girl victims, and perhaps the most common finding about the incestuous father from this group of studies is the domineering, authoritarian style in which he relates to his family. He is seen as rigid and moralistic, and demands complete obedience. His impulse control is seen as impaired, *particularly in family matters,* and some report that he may exhibit "restricted psychopathy" in connection with the incestuous behavior while function-ing in a well-adjusted manner in the community. A variety of psychiatric diagnoses have been given to the fathers, but there is little agreement about them.[6]

Most incestuous fathers are autocratic, but *autocratic* does not necessarily mean powerful or in control. Father may be perceived as a tyrant; yet his power may be questionable. For example, some cases of abuse involve fathers who are mouselike and fearful of their own sexuality, so they choose children who cannot resist them. This type of father may be married to a strong, domineering woman who is in denial regarding her own sexual drive and who sexually (and possibly even relationally) shuts out the father.

In this latter situation it may be Mother who is the real source of power in the family system. Yet to the child's eye, Father may have the appearance of being powerful, especially as he dominates the victim sexually. Some weak men marry strong women, then seek out weak females to meet their sexual needs.

There are many clinical diagnoses of perpetrators that could apply. One might guess, for example, the presence of a compulsive or obsessive-compulsive personality disorder. Disorders of impulse control in general are almost certainly present. One of many psy-chosexual disorders may apply. One might suspect an adjustment or anxiety disorder. And substance abuse disorders are frequently associated with sexual abuse. Sanford indicates that alcohol plays a part in 60 percent of sexual abuse incidents, and her study did not include any other controlled substances such as cocaine, crack, speed, or heroin. In some cases a diagnosis of sociopath may be in order. One would almost always expect poor socialization to be part of the diagnosis.

While it is not pleasant for a victim to speculate that her family-member perpetrator suffered from some clinical disorder, she may need to know that sexual abuse *is* pathologically rooted. Abuse is *not* something that a normal, healthy, well-balanced family man does.

If Father is the perpetrator, he may be making a very angry statement against his wife, choosing his daughter over his wife. There are few more humiliating experiences for a woman than having her daughter chosen as a sexual partner over herself.

If a brother or some other nonparental male is the perpetrator, both parents may be passive and unable or unwilling to stand up to the abuser. In this case both parents may have their own sexual hang-ups and may create an atmosphere in which conversation regarding anything sexual is prohibited.

When Grandfather is the abuser, some family systems attempt to protect him by claiming that he is so old that he doesn't know what he is doing. They joke about it rather than defending the victim.

When an uncle or cousin is the abuser, some victims feel that speaking up about the abuse would jeopardize intrafamilial relationships. Note that in not speaking up, the victim becomes the protector of the abuser.

From out of a murky fog, answers begin to form. The victim is isolated from help. Mother doesn't step in to help; she is absent, incompetent, or unapproachable. If Father is not the abuser, he is either incompetent or unapproachable. In short, the family system is dysfunctional, and the victim becomes one of the carriers of the sickness. Fossum and Mason state, "The incest family maintains their shame by the abusing father, a denying mother, a powerfully victimized and burdened daughter, and the guilt-and-fear-ridden siblings."[7]

OTHER FAMILY DYNAMICS

Role Reversals

In some abusive systems the victim replaces Mother as the "adult" female (sexual partner) in the family. The child becomes the wife, and the wife becomes the child. When this happens the child can end up mothering her own mother, wielding power and authority beyond her years. The girl grows up too quickly, for obvious reasons.

In this case the reversal is not usually total, permanent, or clear. This reversal serves a purpose that may change from day to day or from hour to hour. At some times the daughter will have Dad's supportive authority to act as the mother. At other times Mother and/or Father will strip the daughter of that authority and require her to be a child. No wonder disorientation results!

Boundary and Power Issues

Boundaries and power issues become obscure and manipulative. Even a mother who has adopted a chronic physical or emotional problem to avoid dealing with incest is still Mother, and from time to time she may assert herself as such. Even a mother who has sacrificed her daughter to her husband may become insanely jealous of her daughter. Therefore, she may alternately treat the girl with pity and hatred, acceptance and rejection, or a weird mixture. And the child who unconsciously attempts to rescue her mother by becoming her father's sexual partner may find herself hating her mother, her father, and herself.

In this chaotic system, the question of who can do what to whom changes often. Today Father can rape Daughter. Tomorrow Mother is angry at Daughter for being a "seductress." The next day Brother may join in the incestual relationship. Then Father may punish Daughter for being sexually active with Brother, or he may punish Brother for being a rival. One day Father may tell Daughter that he loves her more than he loves Mother. The next day Mother may be back in the leading role as head female. It is a fluid cycle full of denial, confusion, and insanity.

Power flows here and then there, seemingly randomly. Boundaries mix and mesh to fit the individuals at the moment of their needs. Identities and roles flex to meet the pathology being acted out at the moment. Through it all the victim is torn, wrenched, and destroyed.

The Family Dictatorship

Not all abusive family systems are chaotic. In some situations the father (or mother) rules with an absolute, total power, dictating to and controlling every person in the family. In this type of system there is only one person holding power, and everyone knows who that is. Still, even within this dictatorship, roles frequently change as the victim moves from being wife/mistress/mother back to being child.

General Powerlessness of Victim

Powerlessness is a major issue for the victim, who is almost always disempowered. Victims frequently say, "I had no one to whom I could have turned. Even if I had told someone, it wouldn't have made any difference. If anything, it would have made things worse for me." Also, in most of these cases, those who might have wished to help either are or perceive themselves to be powerless.

Inability to Deal with Bad News

The family system that doesn't help the victim usually exhibits an inability to tolerate or deal with bad news. For example, if someone brings home a bad report card, the grades are not discussed. If someone puts a dent in the family car, the damage is not mentioned. Or there is so much anger or violence that the message is well learned for the future: don't bring painful things out into the open. Keep them hidden. If this is true of a report card or a dented fender, how much more true it is of sexual abuse!

Keeping Secrets

Keeping secrets becomes a way of life for many victims, especially if they come from incestuous homes. The situation makes sense to the family: Victim can't tell Mother because Mother is, for whatever reason, unavailable for help. Mother won't confront Father, both for her reasons and his. Father won't go for help because that would be an admission of guilt, and he might be put in jail. So nobody talks about anything meaningful.

Claudia Black identifies three rules that exist when families deny the reality of their dysfunction and pain: don't talk, don't trust, and don't feel.[8] In order to process and heal an abusive situation, one must talk about it! Dysfunctional family systems don't allow victims to talk about their pain.

"Don't trust" becomes a by-product. How can a person trust another person when being abused and/or left to her own powerlessness? How can one trust the very ones who should be stopping the abuse?

"Don't feel" becomes a life-style. Denial of feelings is pervasive among most victims. And why not! Denial of feelings was a survival technique at one point in her life and is naturally carried into adulthood. It's safer not to feel.

Meanwhile, most victims learn to keep their secrets well hidden.

And what better soil within which to bury painful secrets than that of "don't talk, don't trust, and don't feel."

The Religious Incestuous Family System

Incest cuts across all socioeconomic, political, educational, and religious lines. In fact, a surprising number of victims come from homes that had the appearance of being deeply religious.

It is important to understand that abusers frequently have rigid personality structures, prone to fitting into religious systems that are also rigid. These individuals, in keeping with their pathology, are adept at finding passages of Scripture that seem to confirm their right to their pathology.

Using the Bible to defend incest is like using it to defend murder, robbery, or perjury. The fact that some people do this type of thing doesn't make it right. They are rationalizing their pathology. No person who knows the least bit about God, His great love for us, and His deep desire for us to be whole in Him would believe for a moment that incest is in any way related to God's will.

Victims may be helped to know that perpetrators who quote God's Word in committing their evil will one day stand before God. According to the Bible these abusers quote, *the whole of created universe* will be watching, and at that point *there will be no more secrets*. Everyone will see what the perpetrator did, and God will indeed judge. (Read Rev. 20:12–15.)

No matter how "religious" a perpetrator may wish to appear, he is a fraud if he has not (a) confessed his sins to God, his victims, and any others he may have wronged; (b) asked for forgiveness from God, his victim, and any others he has wronged; (c) stopped the abuse; and (d) done all in his power to make amends to the victim and any others who may have been affected by his sins. Pay no attention to his claims of religion; they are meaningless.

The Shame-Bound Family System

Fossum and Mason outline a dynamic that they call the "shame-control model of abusive family interaction."[9] Although shame is a constant companion of the abuse victim, many family systems within which abuse occurs are also bound and controlled by shame.

Often this very shame is used to control the victim and to lead her into further abuse.

THREE THEORIES ABOUT INCESTUOUS FAMILY SYSTEMS

Social Theory

This approach highlights factors such as socioeconomic class, poverty, overcrowding, and social or geographical isolation as being primarily responsible for conditions that lead to incest.

While the concept of social isolation may have some merit in that girls who are sexually abused are frequently isolated from sources of help, much of this theory does not hold up under scrutiny. Sexual abuse occurs across all socioeconomic strata, not only at poverty levels or in rural areas.

The overcrowding factor in such assumptions could also be used to argue against the prevalence of abuse. An overcrowded home might not provide an abuser with the opportunity to be alone with a child or to shape a family system within which secrets are easily held.

Psychodynamic Theory

The superego, id, and ego are Freudian terms meaning, basically, one's conscience, lower urge drives, and adult mediating processes, respectively. In a healthy adult, the ego mediates between the superego and the id, keeping the person from being overly rigid (controlled by the superego) or completely impulse driven (controlled by the id).

Some theorists speculate that the intrafamily male who sexually abuses is a domineering individual with a weak ego, who perhaps is subconsciously expressing rage against his mother or his wife. The perpetrator may also have regressed to a lower level of functioning than his biological age would suggest.

Within this theoretical approach, even if there is a rigid superego in place, the impulses of the id are not sufficiently directed by the ego. This factor may explain the frequent appearance of a rigid personality structure that is wildly out of control. Some would speculate that the ego is so weak that there may be little real sense of self in the perpetrator and that this limited sense of self is enhanced by dominating a victim.

This theory has its merits; and it too explains a part of the dynamics of sexual abuse. Yet problems remain. When a male in a family sexually violates a female child, the issue is often larger than one individual acting alone. Often other family members play covert supportive roles, and there are almost always severe repercussions throughout the entire family system. These repercussions can last for generations.

Family Systems Theory

Within this approach, abuse and incest are seen as being a whole family problem—something to be treated as a system rather than as a single individual problem. This approach has further advantages in that it seems to deal most effectively with the multigenerational aspects of incest. Questions asked within this approach include:

- How could one family member sexually abuse another?
- Why did the mother choose to marry a man who would have the tendency to sexually abuse a daughter?
- Why does the perpetrator seem to ignore the painful legacy he is inflicting on his victim?
- Why does the whole family seem to turn its head away from the victim's behavioral or verbal cries for help?
- How is it possible that there is no set of agreed-upon rules that govern every family member's behavior toward one another?
- How can one person dominate a whole group of individuals and destroy several lives?
- Why is everyone else so powerless?

These are *family* questions. Repetitive abuse and/or incest do not happen in a vacuum. Hence, the family systems approach to abuse often provides answers to many deep questions when one is attempting to make sense of and heal from sexual abuse. The motto of the family systems theory is a good one: "By the family wounded; by the family healed." The best healing is the most broad-based, interpersonal, intergenerational healing, in which *everything* is brought into the light of day, repented of, forgiven, and reconciled.

THE SCAPEGOAT

In the Old Testament there was a tradition in which once a year the priest would lay his hands upon the head of a goat, repeat the sins of the nation of Israel, symbolically place those sins onto the goat, and then send the goat into the wilderness to die. (Read Lev. 16:5–22.)

Such is the case in many victims' lives. Many victims feel as if they are somehow responsible for the pathology of their family system. They have a feeling of carrying the sins of the family or of being turned out of their families. And many families unjustly blame one member for all of the family problems, as if the family would have been perfect without her.

QUESTIONS FOR REFLECTION

1. Reflect upon the role your mother took or did not take in dealing with your abuse.

2. What power-related issues were out of order within your family system?

3. If you are an incest victim, what different roles did you play within your family?

4. What terms from this chapter would you use in describing your family system to a complete stranger?

5. Were you the family scapegoat? In what ways have the shame and sin of the family been heaped onto you?

6. How did your family teach you to keep secrets?

≡ *ACTION ITEMS* ≡

1. Draw a picture that shows the kinds of relationships that existed within your family system. Use colors or symbols for each family member. When you're finished with the picture, show it to someone and describe each color and symbol.

2. Next draw a family tree. Include on that tree every relative you remember. Beside each name write a characteristic of which

you are aware. For example, beside Grandpa Jones's name you might write *angry, controlling, workaholic*; Grandma Jones—*sad, quiet, always giving in, possibly an alcoholic, rigid religion*; Uncle Willie—*like Grandpa Jones but worse, drank a lot, divorced*; Aunt Kate—*intelligent, self-assertive, proper, left Uncle Willie.*

Explore the various relationships that existed between your relatives for the past two to three generations. What you're constructing is called a *genogram*. It's a way for you to understand some of the dynamics of your family system, to help you make some sense out of how you might have ended up living in this system.

Was there any abuse on either side of the family tree within the past three generations? Any alcoholism? Drug abuse? Divorce? Addictive behavior of any kind? As you work on this project try to gain insight into how dysfunctional families get started and how they are maintained.

Work on tracing your origins. If you are able, ask questions of family members. Do as much detailed investigation of your family tree as possible.

FOR SPIRITUAL GROWTH

Read Joshua 5:10–13. As the nation of Israel finally entered the promised land, God stopped giving them free food (manna, which until then had fallen from the sky). The message at that point was twofold: (a) They had arrived home, and (b) they were now responsible for providing their own food.

Part of the healing process that abuse victims must eventually undertake is to accept that they have moved past the time when someone else was responsible for them. They are now adults and have arrived in the "promised land" of self-care. Also, they must learn to provide for their own emotional needs, much as Israel had to begin providing for its own food needs.

What does the image of *arriving home* conjure up in your adult mind as you reflect upon your arrival into adulthood? What would it mean for you to begin taking the responsibility of self-nurturing? If you could go back in time and nurture yourself as a child, how would you help that child to heal?

Chapter 9
Sexual Abuse and Splitting

As I healed, I began to recognize that I am not the bad person I used to think I was. And I began to recognize that my abuser was very, very evil!

When a little girl is sexually molested, the situation is very confusing, often frightening, and usually embarrassing. The little girl is faced with a very difficult choice. Either she is good and the abuser is very bad, or the abuser is good and she is very bad. But it is very unlikely that she would perceive the perpetrator as being good, the abuse as good, and she herself as good.

Somewhere in the abusive situation her natural sense of right and wrong emerges, and she recognizes that something bad is happening. This realization is almost universal. No matter what her age, the little girl intuitively recognizes that something is wrong in the abusive situation.

One victim was sexually abused at about age three or earlier. It's significant (and very healthy!) that she is able to recall the abusive situation. Even at that age, she realized that what was happening was not right.

WHO'S THE BAD GUY?

Recall the options. The abuser is bad, or the victim is bad. The victim will probably not perceive both victim and abuser as good. The little girl will probably see herself as being bad. After all, as we have learned, the abuser is probably some adult whom she knows and cares for.

The child has a dilemma. If almost anyone perceived as being adult—therefore, good—is abusing the little girl, then that adult must be right. He must be good. He must be acting in the child's best interests. After all, aren't all adults supposed to care for children? Aren't all adults supposed to do what is right and good? Aren't all children taught to obey adults, under the assumption that what they request or order is the right thing?

So the little girl's choices are limited. Could it be possible that known, friendly Mr. Abuser is really a bad person? Surely not. Furthermore, Mr. Abuser might have told her that if she gives away their secret, she'll be bad—or he'll kill her mommy.

These possibilities are overwhelming to her young, sensitive personality. So she does a mental flip-flop, assuming that she is bad. Mr. Abuser probably reinforces that message. Perhaps he tells her she is seductive. Perhaps he blames her for his inability to control his own sexual appetite. Perhaps he tells her that he's really doing her a favor by showing her what she'll need to know when she's a big girl.

Whatever the twisted message is, many a victim assumes that the perpetrator is really a nice person and that she, the victim, is really a bad person. And in the event that the abuse might have stimulated her sexually (as it can do, despite the context), she may *really* feel bad about herself.

THE PROCESS OF SPLITTING

The little girl may figuratively split off part of herself. Her goodness "leaves" her, perhaps even becoming attached to the abuser. The abuser's badness "leaves" him and becomes attached to her.

She now feels better. Although this is a twisted reality, she has some control over the uncontrollable. She is bad; and since bad things happen to bad people, a bad thing has happened (or continues to happen) to her. There is justice after all. It makes some sense again.

She feels better until her cognitive processes, her ability to think clearly and use adult mental functions, begin to override her memories and feelings. Then there is mental conflict. Yet she has learned what to do with internal, mental conflict. If she forces it out of her mind, it won't confuse her anymore. So she represses this confusion.

In this state of being split, she often finds herself doing things she doesn't like or believe in. Some victims become dramatically promiscuous. After all, they're only good for sex. After all, they have already given up everything there is to give up, right? After all, they are bad, and bad people do bad things, right? Although this is distorted logic, it has the appearance of making some sense.

Even if the girl is not actively participating in morally wrong or bad situations, often she still has the feeling that something about her is dirty or bad. Some victims go through life looking for the tiniest flaws in themselves. In this way they can convince themselves that they are, indeed, rotten people. This may partially account for many victims' desire for perfectionism. The message is, "I must try very hard to be perfect, because I am actually a very bad person."

Yet there remains the uncomfortable thought that perhaps she's not *all* bad. Perhaps there is some small part of her that might be a little bit good. When that thought creeps out of her subconscious, it is uncomfortable and to be denied, because "she was bad. She did naughty things with Mr. Abuser. She should be punished."

This childhood message often becomes a life message. Many victims live their adult lives as if they are very bad people.

Obviously, splitting will color attitude, perception, and behavior. If, deep inside, a victim believes she's an evil person, then her attitude toward life will reflect that. She will perceive herself, her relationships, and every piece of her life as if she's bad. And her behavior will reflect her attitudes and perceptions.

We've already discussed promiscuity as one response to sexual abuse. Some women go to the other side of the sexual spectrum and become superreligious, denying all forms of sexual thought and activity. These women are also affected by splitting in that they may become quite fearful of sex in general. After all, the last time they were sexually active the format was one in which they perceived themselves to be immoral, inappropriate, and bad. Therefore, every time they think about sex in any way, they have feelings of being bad. Through splitting they have adopted a mentality of being evil, and their subsequent denial of any sexual thought or activity is a reflection of that splitting. The internal message of these women is, "I don't want to be bad, so I need to completely stay away from sex."

Religion and "Reality Shifting"

It is no surprise that many sexual abuse victims turn to religion. Sherri, a seminary student, says that a high percentage of the women in her seminary are victims. "Why would so many women who are victims go to seminary?" she asks.

Obviously, all female victims of sexual abuse don't end up in seminary. But many turn to religion in some form. The reason isn't too hard to understand. If a little girl feels dirty and stained, to what or to whom may she turn in order to help get clean again? If not to God, then there is no one.

If splitting has made a little girl assume that she is basically bad and that the perpetrator is basically good, then a shift in reality has occurred within her personality. In order for her to heal, another shift in reality back to the truth must occur. Only then will the victim be able to see life as it really is. Only then will she be able to see herself as she really is.

That shift in reality is most fully captured by a clear understanding of right and wrong, as defined by God in the Bible. The Bible presents a framework for universal good and evil. It is the ultimate source of and definition for justice and injustice.

The Bible says (read Lev. 20:1–5) that those who abuse children are to be stoned to death. (Aha! Maybe *he* was wrong!) The Bible also says (read John 8:3–11) that one woman was set up to be trapped by some religious fanatics. When she was caught in the act of adultery and brought to Christ, He forgave her. (Aha! Then maybe there's forgiveness for me!) The Bible says (read 1 John 1:9) that there is hope, cleansing, and restoration for anyone who seeks it.

THE PROCESS OF UNSPLITTING

To end the splitting process, to shift back to the reality of who is good and who is bad, two tools will be helpful to victims. The first tool is entrance into a therapy program with a well-trained, Christian, pro-woman counselor. The second tool—one of the most effective methods of help possible—is for the victim to find a *genuine* holy woman, tell her story, and allow the Christian woman to grieve and weep with her, hold her in her arms, and accept her unconditionally.

Keep in mind that Mother was probably not there for the victim. And perpetrators are ingenious about breaking the bond between the child and parent(s). The little girl was isolated from the source of help that should be available at all times to children: parents.

Women victims need somehow to find Mother. In a few cases this could be one's own blood mother. In cases where this is not possible, a mature, good, spiritual woman may be willing to temporarily adopt this role.

It may sound silly, but it can be immensely healing for a victim to sense another woman's grief at what has happened in her life. To see another woman ("Mother") brought to tears by her story; to feel the friend's extreme anger at the perpetrator; to sense love and total acceptance freely given by a loved one—all of this helps the victim restore a small degree of right and wrong in her heart.

Ultimately, to end the splitting, the victim must go to God and accept God's immeasurable love. One of the most healing and sanity-producing exercises that a split victim can do is to spend time with God, praying, reading Scripture, and learning God's evaluation of her.

Unfortunately, this is something that most victims are unable to accomplish alone because they continue to interpret love—even God's—through the eyes of a stained and evil victim. They stay split.

Therefore, it is important for victims to be in contact with Christian women who know everything about them, who will continue to work at reinforcing the love of God in the victims' hearts and minds. There is a need for mature Christian women to become involved in the lives of sexual abuse victims, for the purpose of demonstrating the love and acceptance of both "Mother" and of God.

QUESTIONS FOR REFLECTION

1. Describe yourself in terms of moral characteristics, first before your abuse and then after. In your own eyes, did you change morally as a result of your abuse? If so, how did you change?

2. How would you define any changes you described in question 1 above, in light of what you have learned in this chapter about splitting?

3. Was your abuser an evil person? If you say anything other than "Yes, he was very evil," then what can you learn about yourself in this chapter regarding splitting?

4. If evil is dynamic—that is, if evil has a life of its own—how did your abuse begin to take hold of your own life?

5. What is your self-talk like? Do you tend to reinforce yourself in positive ways ("Way to go, you did well this time!") or in negative ways ("Way to go, stupid—you blew it again!")? If you choose the latter, what does that type of reinforcement tell you about your own splitting?

≡ ACTION ITEMS ≡

1. Make a list of moral characteristics that you had prior to your abuse. Then draw up a list of moral characteristics that have been true of you since your abuse. If there is any difference between the two lists, write two paragraphs regarding how you have split and what you intend to do to shift your reality back to normal.

2. List twenty moral characteristics that you wish to have.

3. List twenty moral characteristics that you do not wish to have (either now or in the future).

4. Write your own name over the first list, and write the name of your perpetrator over the second list. (Note: This may or may not be an accurate portrayal of either yourself or your abuser. But it will help you see how to unsplit some pieces of yourself and your

perpetrator that may have become inappropriately attached to one another.)

FOR SPIRITUAL GROWTH

1. Write a prayer for yourself. In it, tell God that you are a victim. Tell Him how you feel about yourself. Ask Him to help cleanse you. Ask Him to give you a strong sense of His deep love for you. Ask Him to help you get rid of any evil notions about yourself that you may have adopted as a result of your abuse.

Chapter 10
Sexual Abuse and Being a Victim

If there is one common trait of most sexually abused women, it is that they feel, think, and act like victims much of the time. They have a sense that life has done them wrong and continues to do them wrong. They fear that if something bad happens to them, they won't be able to stop it. They have a feeling that something bad is out there, it's eventually going to happen to them, and when it does they will be powerless.

BEING A VICTIM

One day Jessica was walking in a park. It was a sunny day, and she was enjoying the lake and the ducks when suddenly a man rode past her on a bicycle and fondled her. The incident was over instantly, but it lingered in Jessica's mind for months. She was angry and once again felt like a victim. The situation underscored her perspective of life: "I usually feel as if life holds many potential bad things in it, and whatever happens to me, well, I probably can't stop it anyway."

Jessica's boss was a surgeon and was extremely vulgar toward her most of the time. She felt powerless, as if she could not say to him, "I don't appreciate it when you are vulgar toward me. I want you to stop it right now, or I'm going to file a complaint with the hospital board."

Many adult victims don't realize that they have the power to stop being victimized. In fact, many victims of sexual abuse go through life actually creating situations for themselves in which they will almost certainly be treated as victims. At the same time they invite victimization and hate being victimized.

Even victims who become angry, nasty, and spiteful are still victims. These women say, "Everyone is out to get me." "If I give anyone an inch, they'll take a mile." "I can't buy a gallon of milk without someone taking advantage of me."

Female sexual abuse victims aren't the only ones who attempt to ameliorate their feelings of victimization by becoming crabby and brittle. I know a man who has felt victimized since he was a child. As he has aged he has become increasingly hostile, crabby, and suspicious. He now lives virtually alone. His wife left him several years ago. His son, who lives in the same community, seldom visits him. He has alienated most of his neighbors. He is retired, so he has no business relationships. He once told me that everyone who knows him hates him and that perhaps he deserves to be hated.

He shares a common fence with another neighbor. Last year he became angry that some children, having a party in the adjacent backyard, had hit a plastic whiffle ball over the fence and had crossed his yard to retrieve it. He retaliated by permanently locking the gate.

He is now so isolated and angry that he seldom leaves the house. He goes for walks in the late evening, but wears a radio headset and walks with his eyes downward, never looking people in the eye or saying hello to them. He is a victim. In all likelihood he will die a victim. Sadly, this is the case with many victims.

COMMON FEELINGS OF VICTIMS

Victims have many common characteristics. Following are some of them.

1. Victims feel that life is negative or dangerous. It's "out there to get them."

2. Victims often feel that they deserve a dangerous or difficult life.

3. Victims feel helpless, powerless to stop being victimized.

4. If victims ever do work up enough courage to act, they often overreact.

5. Then victims feel further alienated and isolated.

6. Victims feel angry when being taken advantage of, even in slight ways.

7. Victims often covertly invite others to treat them badly, then resent being treated badly.

8. In many cases victims carry a great deal of old anger, but seldom think or talk about it.

9. Victims usually go through life feeling and presenting themselves as "one down."

10. Victims usually feel that what happened to them long ago has little or no bearing upon what is happening to them now.

PSYCHOSOMATIC ILLNESS AND VICTIMIZATION

Most victims don't realize that they are acting and thinking like victims. Many victims report stomach ailments or frequent headaches. Some have frequent bouts with psychosomatic illness. These are not fake illnesses. They are *real* illnesses, caused primarily by psychological issues. Examples of psychosomatic illnesses can include frequent headaches, migraine headaches, acid stomach, colitis, high blood pressure, heart problems, respiratory problems, including asthma, frequent cold/flu, and general susceptibility to illnesses.

Being a victim requires vigilance. Since both vigilance and unresolved feelings keep the body in a relatively constant state of being hyperalert, issues common to victims form roots for psychosomatic illnesses. One woman underwent major surgery to remove part of her stomach. She had been having strong stomach pain for so many years that finally she and her doctors decided to take out the ailing part.

THE LIFE OF A VICTIM

When a child is being beaten, fondled, raped, or abused in any manner, that child is being victimized. The child is in a situation that is out of control, inappropriate, frightening, and confusing. The child internalizes many of the following messages. "Life is not safe." "I cannot trust the people I wish to love." "I feel out of control, crazy, violated." "I must be very bad to be treated like this." "This is terribly confusing." "I feel shameful." "There is no help nearby to save me." "What I think and feel must be wrong." "I deserve being treated badly." "I am afraid." This list will give you a slight idea of the huge, overwhelming messages that can flood a child's mind during and after abuse.

Now magnify these messages by 100,000. Hear the child scream silently in a dark room where nobody hears. Then leave her alone in the dark closet, and let her grow for the next ten or twenty years. Only you and she know that she lives in that dark closet. The rest of the world sees her as normal. She sees herself as ugly. Now she's an adult. And her life is a reflection of abuse.

Adult women who are sexual abuse victims carry the marks on their souls. They walk into the "room" of life like every other woman, but the dark closet of their souls and the scars are ever with them.

THE GIRL TIED TO THE BED

One victim was tied, hands and feet, to four bedposts and raped multiple times at a fraternity party. Some victims can identify with this. Often they go through life as if they are still tied to the bedframe, naked, vulnerable. They feel powerless, helpless, and angry.

In counseling I often use this ugly picture as an analogy to help victims understand that they are able to untie the cords and chase away the one who tied them up.

It sounds so simple as one reads it, but this is a difficult part of the core of recovery. Most victims feel that they have no option but to remain tied to the bedpost.

EFFECTS OF ABUSE IN ONE'S SOUL

Some women come into life with stronger self-esteem than others. Some women have a grandmother who loved them, and they are able to draw upon that love as they work on their own recovery. Some women marry men who are supportive, tender, and caring. Some women earn advanced degrees in psychology and thereby learn how to heal. Some women turn to the church or go to seminary, and therein learn of God's love for them.

But as a general rule, sexual abuse is deeply pervasive, powerfully affective, and as stubborn as an India ink stain upon fresh white cotton. Recovery is possible, but it takes time and lots of hard work. It takes being brave and being willing to face lots of crummy emotions. It takes believing that you are worth all the hard work.

One major step in recovery involves the victim's learning that although she has been tied to the bedpost, she has the *power* to untie the knots. She has the *right* to self-worth. She has the *strength* to say no. She has the *courage* to face even the most distasteful memories. She has the *freedom* to use her legitimate, healthy, and powerful anger to protect herself, in any and all situations and relationships.

QUESTIONS FOR REFLECTION

1. In your own words, describe how a little girl grew up to be an adult victim.

2. What does being a victim feel like? What does it feel like to be violated? Use as many "feeling" words as possible, and be as complete in your description as your mind will allow.

3. How many of the words you used to answer question 2 have become themes in your own life? How many of them represent the way you face life and the way you handle adult relationships?

4. Why do victims often continue being victims?

5. What does a person have to do in order to stop being a victim?

6. How does your answer to question 5 apply to your adult life and relationships?

≡ *ACTION ITEMS* ≡

1. Make a list of your five most significant current relationships. Beside each name write three ways in which you may invite that person to treat you as a victim.

2. Ask your two closest friends if there are ways in which you appear to them to be somewhat victimlike.

3. Beside each word that you listed in question 2 in the Questions for Reflection section, write an antidote. For example, if you used the word *helpless*, then an antidote word might be *powerful* or *capable*.

4. Write a short story about how a victim got away. How did she escape? How did she then stay out of the grasp of her perpetrator? How did she fare in future relationships with men? With women? And what are her strongest personality characteristics now that she's free?

FOR SPIRITUAL GROWTH

1. Read John 19. Do you think that Christ ever felt like a victim? If so, in what ways? Record your answers on paper.

2. Christ was probably crucified naked, and He was nailed and tied down. In what ways could He identify with your feelings of being an abuse victim? Write your answers.

3. Could you trust another victim with your deepest memories and thoughts?

Chapter 11
Recognizing Anger

Anger is a common and normal residual effect of sexual abuse. As victims begin to heal they experience anger. Perhaps the word *anger* is too mild to describe what many recovering victims feel: bitterness, rage, hatred, abhorrence, loathing, and fury. For victims, all of these emotions are normal and healthy.

Victims often deny their anger, repress it, or at least underestimate its strength. To increase victims' self-awareness, we will spend some time discussing anger.

SOCIETY'S PROHIBITION AGAINST FEMALE EXPRESSION OF ANGER

In our society there is a difference in how males and females are taught to handle anger. Although these differences are in the process of changing, boys have traditionally been encouraged to express anger and aggression. Boys have been given such covert messages as "If you're sad, turn your sorrow into aggression. If you're afraid, turn your fear into anger. If you're in pain, ignore it. Just become aggressive."

Girls have traditionally been given different messages. When a little girl is angry enough to hit her friend, her mother or father has been apt to chide her for her aggression. But the girl is encouraged to dissolve into her parent's arms and cry. Thus she learns to deny her feelings of anger and aggression and to transform them into expressions of fear and sadness.

Whereas boys learn to turn fear and sadness into anger and aggression, girls learn to turn anger and aggression into fear and sadness. These patterns continue into adulthood. Consequently, women often have a difficult time both experiencing and expressing anger.

OTHER REASONS WHY VICTIMS AVOID THEIR OWN ANGER

Fear of Its Depth and Power

There are other reasons why women tend to avoid expression of their anger. A common reason is that many women unconsciously recognize the depth of their anger and fear losing emotional control. One woman had to work for several months in individual therapy just to be able to say aloud, with vocal intensity, "I am angry! You hurt me!"

Even though it is reasonable and normal for a victim to be angry with her abuser, it is not at all unusual to find victims denying their anger and, instead, expressing fear and sadness. Some victims report feeling as if they are about to explode with pent-up emotion; yet they deny their anger. Other victims experience high blood pressure, colitis, depression, migraine headaches, and so on, but never make the connection.

The fear of losing control when processing anger can be very powerful. In fact, some victims fear that they will rush for a weapon and attempt murder, suicide, or self-mutilation.

Helplessness

Helplessness is another reason many victims avoid dealing with their anger. Some ask, "What's the use? What possible good could come of rehashing all that painful stuff anyway? Why bother stirring it up again?" They are saying in effect, "No matter what I may feel, there is no hope of healing. I am helpless, just as I was when I was being abused."

Desire to Keep Peace

Another reason some victims suppress their anger is to avoid harming other family members. "Keep the peace" seems to be the motto of many incest victims. "Fake it at family reunions." "Be nice. Don't make waves."

Personal Denial

Sometimes it's easier to live with a bad toothache than to risk going to the dentist, feeling the needle, hearing the drill, tasting the blood, and so on. In the short run, victims often think it is easier to deny their anger and pain than it is to seek healing.

Family Denial

More often than not, abusive family systems work diligently at maintaining denial. If a victim tells the truth and expresses anger about her abuse, she may risk even further alienation from a dysfunctional family system.

SOME WAYS ANGER IS MISHANDLED

Performance Compensation

Many victims are overachievers. Often their anger provides the energy and drive to overachieve, to be perfect. On the other hand, some victims are underachievers. Their anger drains away their energy and motivation.

Transference

One victim reported being edgy and touchy most of the time. Although she loved her husband and children dearly, she frequently found herself snapping at them. Once she began dealing with her childhood abuse and her anger, she realized that she was redirecting her anger at her abusers into "safer" relationships. That's *transference*. As she was able to identify and express her anger at her abusers, she felt less anger toward her loved ones and became a more loving wife and mother.

Projection

Another victim felt that almost everyone in the world was crabby and angry at her. She became reclusive and defensive. In dealing with her own abuse she recognized that the qualities she thought others were displaying toward her were the ones she felt inside. That's *projection*.

Over- or Under-Sexualization

Some victims become immensely promiscuous. Promiscuity can be a complex phenomenon including elements of overcoming loneliness, anxiety about one's body, or lack of self-worth. It can be laced with desires for control and for expressions of anger. Conversely, some women's anger makes them avoid anything remotely sexual. When they approach their own sexuality, they also approach their own anger. For some victims it's easier to deny both.

The "defense mechanisms" we've just discussed exist to help a person remain in denial. Following are a few more of these mechanisms.

- Repression: Force it from all conscious thought.
- Suppression: Just don't think about it much.
- Underrating: Pretend it's not significant now that you're a mature adult.
- Rationalization: Explain it all away.
- Theologize: Tell yourself that God will make it all go away so

you don't have to deal with it. Or tell yourself that being angry is unchristian.

• Flight: Run away from everything. Perhaps even develop some phobias in self-defense.

SOME SYMPTOMS OF MISHANDLED ANGER

Anger is not an emotion to be trifled with. It can be a very powerful dynamic, providing immense, almost unextinguishable energy for years. But it does so at a cost. Three major costs are listed next.

Depression

Unresolved deep anger frequently leads to clinical depression. This is not the type of depression that one feels at the death of a favorite goldfish. Rather, it is a profound inner inability to go on. It can involve an overwhelming loss of energy. It is the feeling that one wishes to remain forever wrapped in a dark and isolated cocoon. It may or may not include deep feelings of sadness or grief. It may include over- or undereating; a desire to sleep all the time; or insomnia. It can involve the loss of desire to groom oneself, clean one's house, and feed one's family.

Physical Illness

Unresolved anger frequently leads to one or more of the following physical ailments: heart disorders (heart attack, high blood pressure); intestinal disorders (ulcer, colitis); breathing disorders (asthma, shortness of breath); major episodic mental/nervous disorders (anxiety attacks, phobias); eating and/or sleeping disorders; headaches, including migraine headaches. There is some limited evidence that even cancer may be somewhat related to emotional stress.

Following is a succinct description of what anger can do to our body.

Many studies show that the stress of anger produces a unique and specific hormonal response that is particularly dangerous. Anger results in elevated levels of testosterone (for men), epinephrine, norepinephrine, and cortisol. Chronic high levels of testosterone and cortisol potentiate atherosclerosis, the most common cause of coronary artery disease. Cortisol also depresses the immune system and reduces the body's ability to fight infection. Epinephrine and norepinephrine stimulate the sympathetic nervous system to shunt blood from the skin, liver and digestive tract to the heart, lungs, and skeletal muscles. Blood pressure is elevated, and glucose is dumped into the blood system to provide energy for confrontation or escape. When blood is shunted away from the liver, the liver is less efficient in clearing the blood of cholesterol, thus contributing to the fatty deposits in the arteries. Elevated blood pressure also damages the arteries and the heart. Hypertension forces the heart to work harder and creates large and less efficient heart muscle. Turbulence caused by high blood pressure of the blood flow also damages the arteries. Tiny tears develop on the artery wall. Fatty deposits cover the tears, but these can eventually grow to fill the artery and stop the flow of blood.

Occasional anger creates no lasting harm, but chronic, sustained anger keeps the body in a constant state of emergency, and the regular body functions, such as digestion, clearing the blood of cholesterol, and resisting infection, may be delayed, depressed, or bypassed. Chronic anger thus contributes to the development of a variety of diseases—digestive disorders, hypertension, heart disease, susceptibility to infections, rashes, headaches, and many more.[1]

LaHaye and Phillips provide a general listing of physical symptoms experienced by patients in a clinic. All of these symptoms can be precipitated by chronic anger: urticaria or hives, eczema, cold and moist hands, runny nose, asthma, diarrhea, constipation, nausea and vomiting, duodenal ulcer, migraine headache, arterial hypertension, and low back pain.[2]

VICTIMS' STATEMENTS ABOUT ANGER

Several women have chosen to share examples of their own anger with you. They follow.

"I walk around in life feeling like I'm ready to either blow up or fall apart in tears! Just the other day I blasted a supermarket cashier for the smallest thing! I can't even remember what the reason was now."

"I can't understand why I feel like crying so much of the time. I'm not sad about anything that I can think of."

"I know I'm a difficult person to live with. I don't know how my husband has put up with me all these years or why I am difficult so often."

"I find myself snapping at my children so much. It's like I need them to be absolutely perfect for me, or I'll clobber them! Why am I so angry?"

"The other day a guy brushed past me, too close. It wasn't an accident. He was trying to feel my body as he brushed past me. I wanted to murder him, literally! But instead I went into the women's room and cried."

Reflect on these statements. All of them are examples of misplaced anger. Now imagine yourself as a pressure cooker. Normally you have a relief valve to allow pressure to escape. However, there are two additional variables: (1) Your parents or society built into you a message that "good girls don't blow off steam"; and (2) because of your abuse the heat under the pressure cooker has been turned to "high" all the years since your abuse.

All this time you have tried to put on a smiling face that tells the world you're just fine. "Oh, sure, something happened to me when I was younger, but that was years ago, and I try not to think too much about it anymore. I feel too emotional and depressed when I think about it."

When a person feels "too emotional" in thinking about a situation, that person has unfinished business. Feelings are *signals*. They have meaning. Like any emotion, anger is a signal. When a pressure cooker begins to build up high pressure, the valve on the top begins to whistle. That's a *signal*. If someone tried to open the lid at that point, there would be an explosion.

Let's extend the metaphor further. Inside that pressure cooker is something rotten. It smells terrible. What are our options? We could ignore the pressure and allow it to continue building, hoping that it doesn't blow up. We can remove the lid and get hurt. Or we can begin letting the pressure out of the pot little by little, with our ultimate goal to get rid of that rotten thing in the pot.

Sexual abuse produces anger. Anger is legitimate. It's a signal. It's OK to be angry. God gave us the emotion of anger, and Christ demonstrated His anger from time to time while on earth.

Victims have many reasons to be angry. Your abuser breached the trust that normally exists between adult and child. You were some person's sexual toy. You lost part of your innocence. You were taught about sex in a way that made it feel dirty and made you feel dirty. You experienced situations that are inappropriate for children. You lost part of your childhood. You were violated. After your abuse, you may have found it difficult to trust people; to maintain close girlfriend relationships; to have healthy male/female relationships; to forgive those who didn't rescue you.

If you are a victim, are you angry? If you are not angry, have you been through enough spiritual and clinical healing that you have finally been able to grow past your anger? Or are you in denial? As you read this chapter, did you see yourself?

QUESTIONS FOR REFLECTION

1. Reflect upon how you were taught to handle your anger versus how your parents handled their anger. Write down five memories you have involving childhood anger and the parental messages that you associate with your memories.

2. Consider how you can associate your anger with stressful situations you experienced in the last week (for example, the supermarket cashier, your children, a dating relationship, your homelife with your husband, feelings about yourself and/or your body). In the past week, has your anger spilled over in spite of your best attempts to contain it?

3. Why do you think God created anger? Can you name three purposes it was created to serve?

4. Why do you think anger is such a frightening emotion for you, as an abused woman, to express? When you were a child, what

happened (or didn't happen) to you when you tried to express anger?

5. How has your anger affected your life as you have attempted close relationships? What role does your anger play within these relationships?

ACTION ITEMS

1. Begin writing a letter to the person(s) who abused you. You will *not* mail this letter, so be explicit. Tell everything that you have experienced as a result of your abuse. Get it *all* out. Write for days if you need to do so. But do not send the letter.

2. Find a place where you can be completely alone, with no possibility of interruptions. Then read your letter aloud as if addressing your abuser. Pour out your feelings, including your anger and your hurt. Tell your abuser all about what he did to you and how it affected you. Scream or cry as much as you wish. Let yourself go. As you walk through this pain, promise yourself that you're *not going to hurt yourself anymore on his account*. You've been hurt enough. Now it's time for healing. The purpose of this exercise is to help you begin to express your anger and to put the weight of responsibility where it belongs—on your abuser.

3. Lie on the floor, on your back, and imagine your abuser approaching you. This time, however, push your hands upward and say repeatedly, "No! You do not have my permission! Stop! Go away!" Then imagine your abuser leaving the room. How does it feel to say *no*? You *may* say it. It's OK to say no to anyone who abuses you in any way.

FOR SPIRITUAL GROWTH

1. Read John 2:13–16 and reflect on the anger of Christ. He allowed himself both to be angry and to express His anger. Can you allow yourself to be angry? Can you allow yourself to express your anger?

2. In Exodus 32:19 Moses was very angry, and he acted out of anger. In this case a very normal human being was angry, and the

incident was recorded in the Bible. Can you allow yourself to have normal, healthy, even deep anger?

3. Ephesians 4:26 says, "Be angry but do not sin" (RSV). What is the difference between being angry and sinning? Does God allow us to be angry? Or do we have to repress our real feelings in order to be accepted by Him?

Chapter 12
Processing Anger

It's one thing to know you're angry. It's much harder to learn how to process anger so that it does not control your life any longer. If you don't believe that you're angry about your abuse, then this chapter won't do much for you yet. You can't get rid of something that you don't realize or admit you have.

The first step in processing anger is admitting that you're angry. For example, picture a man coming home from work, having just been told by his boss that he's getting a 30 percent cut in pay. The man knows the cut is a "punishment." An employee in another department made the mistake, but he's being blamed for it. As he walks through the door his wife takes one look at his face and says, "Are you angry about something?" If he says, "Yes, I am really mad!" then together they can process the unfair experience.

However, suppose he screams at her, "No, stupid! I'm not mad! I always look this way when I come home from the office!" Then there's not much they can talk about. She's shut out. Worse, she's now the focus of his misplaced anger. Following are some suggestions for processing anger.

NAME YOUR FEELINGS

In chapter 11 several legitimate reasons for anger were given. To process your anger you must be able to specifically identify the reasons for your anger. Right now, while you're thinking about it, write your own list of reasons why you're angry.

1. _____
2. _____
3. _____
4. _____
5. _____
6. _____
7. _____
8. _____
9. _____
10. _____

As you name your anger, *be very specific.* Victims often tend to be vague. Following are some examples of specific versus vague naming of anger.

Vague	*Specific*
1. I'm angry about my childhood sexual abuse.	I'm angry that Uncle Ned tricked me into letting him fondle and undress me.
2. I'm angry at Mom for not doing anything to help me.	I'm angry with Mom because I think she knew I was being raped, and she didn't do anything to help or protect me. She never even talked with me about it.

Vague	*Specific*
3. I'm hurt because of what Billy did to me.	I'm hurt and angry because Billy raped me on our fifth date, and I was starting to trust him. Now I have a hard time trusting men at all. Whenever I start thinking about sex I see Billy's face. He's ruined lots of things that should be special.
4. I'm angry with Dad for things he did to my sister and me.	I'm angry with Dad because he touched me and made me touch him. I was embarrassed and humiliated. And I'm angry because he did the same things with my little sister. I despise my own father.

EXPRESS YOUR FEELINGS

Doesn't it sound simple? "Express your feelings." No problem, right? But for victims this is often an immense challenge because feelings are the very last thing they wish to face. A few specific tasks can be helpful.

DESCRIBE YOUR FEELINGS

At the end of this chapter is a list of feelings. If you have some strong emotion and can't identify it, read the list and choose the feeling that seems right. Remember, many abuse victims have learned to deny their feelings or to transfer their feelings from one type to another. Victims tend to be out of touch with much of what they feel. So name your feelings; be specific; write them down.

JOURNAL YOUR FEELINGS

If a person's skin is seriously burned, after sufficient time the wound will stop hurting. The skin will probably heal enough for the person to have more or less normal feelings on that burned area. But the mind is more complex. When deeply wounded the mind can convince itself that it is not wounded. The pain may mysteriously disappear. However, pain of the magnitude resulting from sexual abuse doesn't just go away. If not addressed it often recedes beneath the surface of conscious thought. But it's still there, pulling strings and affecting perception, attitude, and behavior.

To process pain of the mind, it is helpful to go back to the place where it was hurt. Remember the pain. Feel it. Let it wash over you. Accept the grief that is associated with it. Accept the losses that come to mind as you experience the anguish.

Tell yourself that it's OK to feel what's real, even if it hurts. Assure yourself that if you accept the pain of your life, and then work at wading through the emotional junk that is associated with the pain, you'll eventually come out on the other side. "To heal it you have to feel it."

Journaling can be very helpful in this process. Recording thoughts on paper seems to involve a different process of self-exploration than does talking about them. One's mind is usually several paragraphs ahead of one's ability to write. While the hand is attempting to scratch out a few words the mind is already reformulating the words, bringing more memory to bear upon the sentence, and fleshing out the experience being written.

As you feel it again, write it down. Be thorough! In this process of journaling you will be using your cognitive, intellectual, adult skills of expression and thought development to help express the physical, emotional, and spiritual pain of a child. You will be using your adult knowledge to help the child within you express things that she was never able to say, feel, or process.

Go back into the swamp. Feel it. Let it be part of you. Then write it down, just as you experienced it, just as you feel it. Let your tears stream as you go back to look at the child being abused. Release your anger. Let your compassion for her overwhelm the memories. Remember, feel, and write.

RECOGNIZE YOUR OWN BOILING POINT

Imagine a pot of water sitting on a stove. The temperature of the pot is 210 degrees Fahrenheit. On another stove nearby is another pot. The temperature of the second pot is 35 degrees Fahrenheit. If we apply equal heat to both pots, which pot will boil over faster?

Victims of any kind frequently carry a lot of anger. They live their lives close to the boiling point. Consequently, only a small escalation of heat is needed to make them boil over.

Part of the healing task involves learning that you may have so much internal anger that you boil over easily. In fact, that recognition in itself might be helpful. Now the task is to learn how to cool down the pot. Following are some tips.

LEARN YOUR OWN TRIGGERS

We all have triggers—certain things that drive us crazy. Some of us have lots of them; others only have a few. Our triggers usually occur at points of personal pain, fear, sadness, or memory. When someone bumps against these triggers, there is often an explosion of some sort. Part of the task of healing is identifying our own triggers and understanding the cycle of anger.

McKay, Rogers, and McKay identify a cycle of anger.[1] It operates as follows:

- *Stress:* Something stresses us. It could be something someone says. It could be the normal pressures of the day. It could be a husband, a boss, a child, a cashier at the supermarket.
- *Trigger thoughts:* We respond to the stress by hitting our trigger thoughts. They usually include some internal message that we repeat to ourselves. These trigger thoughts usually have two characteristics: blame and "shoulds." We blame others for the problems we face, and we tell ourselves that they should or should not do certain things.
- *Anger:* Then we get mad. We go through the cycle again: trigger (blame, shoulds), anger, trigger, anger, and so on.

To break this cycle we must be willing to accept that life is not always fair, that people don't always do the right thing, and that life still goes on. We have to decide upon what level of anger we choose to allow to exist within *ourselves.* How sour do you want life to taste?

RECOGNIZE THE INTERPERSONAL COSTS OF YOUR ANGER

The decision to unload your anger is often easier when you realize what it's doing in your relationships with those you love. Anger usually keeps you away from love—from either giving or receiving it. Anger usually isolates you. As time passes, you begin to realize that your decision to hold onto your anger is very costly. You recognize that you have a choice to make.

RECOGNIZE ANGER AS YOUR CHOICE

Anger is a choice, a right, a natural emotion. It is often used as a source of internal fuel. It can give the illusion of power. It can be a means of help in certain difficult situations. But chronic anger is a choice.

My grandmother decided to be angry most of the time. She had common anger symptoms, including asthma, a low boiling point, and isolation from meaningful relationships. I have no idea why she chose to be angry most of the time. I only know I didn't like being around her. She died with only one relationship. The choice to hold onto anger costs a great deal in relationships.

LEARN TO MEET YOUR OWN NEEDS

Many victims stay angry because they don't accept their responsibility to meet their own needs. As children, when they were abused they learned that they could not meet their needs for safety, privacy, and control. It's hard to unlearn the message of helplessness.

The message can last well into adulthood. It can become a life theme. And when one is constantly unable to meet her own needs, she becomes very frustrated. Many victims live with anger that seems out of control because they do not realize their own ability to take control.

Some victims realize their ability, but fear taking control or asserting their will. It can feel really good to stick out your arm at what seems to be an oncoming tank, firmly say "Stop!" and watch the machine actually begin to stop!

RECOGNIZE YOUR OWN ANGER "HABIT"

Anger can be addictive, an acquired habit. People can be so used to facing life with angry faces that they forget how to approach life without anger. Anger sometimes becomes a habit because it gives a person a sense of power. But if one uses anger too often, it would be helpful to explore the reasons why.

Victims have every right to be angry. If they don't admit and process their own anger, they can be trapped by it forever. There is a time to let it go and to forbid it to ruin the remaining years of life.

STOP ESCALATION OF ANGER

To get past anger one must be willing to stop escalating. That may mean feeling as if one has lost the battle. But there's a larger perspective worth noting. Ongoing battles keep us mentally engaged with people, usually in a dysfunctional manner. There comes a time to walk away and say, "I'm not fighting any longer. I'm not going to be your victim anymore. If you want to fight, you're on your own. I'm seeking peace for myself."

INTENTIONALLY CHANGE YOUR RESPONSES TO ANGER

Did you know that you could intentionally change your response to anger-producing situations? Try it. The next time you want to kick a wall, try laughing about it. Or sing a song. Or recite some poetry. This technique is not a denial of anger. Rather, it is an adult coping mechanism to help defeat chronic knee-jerk anger. It is possible to choose a different response to a situation than you may have chosen in the past. This option gives you control over your own response. If you're feeling stuck in your own anger trap, perhaps the time has come for you to purposefully and intentionally change your response to your anger.

STOP USING ANGER AS A DEFENSE

When you were being abused as a child, you needed more anger than you were able to muster or were allowed to use. As you matured, you may have learned that anger could be a pretty good defense. It kept people from victimizing you. If you haven't learned this yet, then you need to.

However, if you are constantly using anger as a defense against almost everything, then it is possible that you have gone too far in the other direction. You can stop using your anger all the time.

Sometimes anger is appropriate. Sometimes it is also appropriate to choose other responses to stress, pain, and fear. If you find that you are chronically using anger as a wall to protect yourself, you might ask yourself if this is how you wish to live for the rest of your life.

We all know someone who's stuck in the past. Crusty, negative, and bitter, she constantly brings up events that happened ten or twenty years ago that hurt her. Her favorite phrase is, "By golly, *that's* not going to happen to *me* again!" Do you want to be like her? Are you so fearful, bitter, or sad that anger is your best source of protection and comfort?

FORGIVE

Forgiveness is often almost out of the question for victims. And most counseling centers won't suggest that you even think about it. But it is potentially the most healing course you can undertake.

The effect of forgiveness is so profound that we have devoted an entire chapter in this book to the subject. Read one quotation taken verbatim from an abuse victim's letter. "I (finally) prayed for my rapist. I forgave him. It was at that point that I was able to accept God's forgiveness for me. It overwhelmed me. In that moment of forgiving him, I found God's forgiveness for me too."

COMMON MISTAKES IN PROCESSING ANGER

The following are a few common mistaken approaches that many victims take as they process their anger.

The Drill Sergeant Approach

Some women learn that they can gain control of at least a part of the chaos inside themselves by becoming "drill sergeants." They attempt to control everything and everybody around them.

The mistake in this approach is that you'll never be able to control enough of your surroundings to relieve the chaos inside of you. It's better to work on calming the internal chaos; then you'll need to exert far less external control.

The Self-Condemnation Approach

Some victims verbally abuse themselves. They have the mistaken notion that punishing themselves will somehow make up for what they feel to be their responsibility (stupidity, vulnerability, and so on) in their abuse.

The problem with this approach is obvious. One can't change the past. No amount of self-abuse or punishment will change what happened. Furthermore, you don't need more abuse, especially coming from yourself. You need self-compassion, self-love, self-acceptance, self-nurturing, self-healing, and self-forgiveness. As you victimize yourself by self-abuse you keep yourself in the role of a victim. Is that what you want?

The Helpless Resignation Approach

Many victims continue to be victims because they don't believe there is any other way to act. They approach life as if they were small whipped puppies, their tail between their legs, expecting every hand that touches them to further whip them. "Might just as well roll over and play dead. I'm going to get kicked anyway." Picture a dog lying on its back, its legs sticking straight up in the air, wearing a sign that says, "Kick me." Is this you?

In this role the woman internalizes all of her anger, but is probably not even aware that she is angry or that she has a right to her own feelings. Are you comfortable with repressing your anger year after year? Is it your only option?

The Martyr Approach

In this role the victim uses a bit of her anger—at least, she draws some attention to the situation by being a martyr. But the role is still one of helplessness, and the victim continues to feel angry. Her anger is directed inward and is only "let out" with tiny hints that something's wrong. "Oh well, I might as well do everything myself. Nobody ever helps me anyway. Here we go again, giving me all the responsibility in the world. Well, I guess nobody else is going to do it, so I'll just have to take it all on myself." *(Sigh.)*

This woman's anger is let out in little wisps of steam as she sighs, complains, and then—tiredly, timidly, or sullenly—does the tasks of the martyr. But it's no fun to constantly "eat" anger.

The Scared Approach

This victim learned that life was scary, and she still acts out the message. She plays everything as safely as possible. She's not going to risk anything ever again! Her anger has been transformed into fear, and now she builds a wall of isolation and a world of "safety."

The Depression Approach

Some abuse victims continue to act out their feelings by being depressed most of the time. These women have neither let go of their pain nor processed their anger. Both are constant companions. To let go of either would almost feel like an act of self-betrayal, for this is the only control they allow themselves to have: keeping pain and anger close. These victims need to be sad. To be happy would be to admit that something horrible happened and then to let go of it. These victims use sadness as an expression of anger. Both keep victims in touch with the abuse.

The Superwoman Approach

"Taa Daa! I am woman, hear me roar! I can do anything and everything. I don't hurt! I'm not sad! Life is my cookie and I'm here to munch it! I can raise ten kids, hold down two full-time jobs, and study for a Ph.D. in my spare time."

Don't ask this woman to sit down and rest. When she slows down she begins to relive her pain, and her feelings come pouring out of her unconscious. So she keeps busy—superbusy, hyperbusy. She accomplishes more in one day than five other women do in a month. People marvel at her. But inside she knows there's been a death; she just won't stop to go to the funeral or to grieve the loss. She uses activity as a drug to keep her from feeling the pain. Her anger provides much of her energy and drive. But she doesn't solve much. She just keeps running.

QUESTIONS FOR REFLECTION

1. Use the list provided in the Appendix at the end of this chapter to help you identify some of your emotions. Circle words that help identify and name your feelings, particularly those relating to your abuse. Focus especially on words that might express some aspect of your anger.

2. Have you used any of the roles explored in this chapter to deny processing your anger (drill sergeant, superwoman, martyr, and so on)? If so, why did you choose that role? What has that role done for you?

3. Why is it necessary to allow feelings to exist? Why not just keep them repressed?

4. Reflect upon the actual feelings you experienced during and after your abuse. Name a few of them. Write them down on paper. Have any of those feelings become themes in your life—things that you repetitively reexperience? Or, on the other hand, have you denied feeling them since your abuse?

5. How can your naming the feelings of your abuse give you any power over them? Reflect upon this. For example, how can saying, "I am afraid and angry," provide you with a better means of personal control and dignity than bursting into tears, running out of a room, or angrily throwing dishes?

6. It's basically true that you will either talk about your feelings or in some way act them out. How have you acted out your feelings of anger about your abuse?

≡ *ACTION ITEMS* ≡

1. During the next several days, make notes about what you felt when you were being abused and what you feel now. Draw comparisons between "then" feelings and "now" feelings. Make personal observations as you see them.

2. Make a small sign for yourself, and put it in a place where you can see it several times a day. The sign will say: *Tell It Like It Is, Baby!*

From now on, tell it like it is. If it's a fish, call it a fish. If it stinks, say, "The fish stinks." If someone says, "Hey, that's my pet fish, you're not supposed to say that the fish stinks," then say, "Well, your pet fish stinks." Start working on telling it like it is, *especially with regard to your own feelings*.

3. Finish writing the following sentences:

a. When I am hurt by someone, from now on I will say to that person:_____

_____.

b. When someone begins putting pressure on me to deny my feelings, from now on I am going to say to that person:_____

_____.

c. The difference between being aggressive and being assertive is:
_____

_____.

4. Write ten reasons why it's OK for you to be angry when you are angry.

5. Name any people who overtly or covertly seem to want to keep you from feeling anger or any other emotion.

6. Write two or three pages about the emotions you had while you were being abused and immediately afterward. Be thorough and concise. Then take these pages to a friend, preferably female, and let her read them.

FOR SPIRITUAL GROWTH

The Old Testament book of Judges, chapters 19–21, contains a brutal story of a woman who was gang-raped and then murdered.

Her male companion slept, safe inside a friend's house, knowing that she was being thus treated! First read the story yourself, preferably in a modern translation. Then reflect upon the following questions.

1. Does the story make you angry? If so, why are you angry? If not, why are you not angry?

2. How was "justice" handled? What more could or should have been done?

3. How many people died in the resulting war?

4. What happened to almost all of the members of the tribe of Dan (men, women, children)?

5. Should a whole tribe including men, women, and children have been wiped out because they would not take responsibility for punishing individuals who raped and murdered the woman? That is, _does a society have a responsibility to punish sexual offenders and murderers? If so, what should happen to that society if it fails to do so?_

6. What should have happened to the man who knew of the abuse, but didn't protect this woman?

FEELING WORDS

Abandoned	Anxious	Beautiful	Callous
Accepted	Apart	Belittled	Calm
Accused	Apologetic	Belligerent	Capable
Aching	Appreciative	Bereaved	Captivated
Adventurous	Apprehensive	Betrayed	Carefree
Affectionate	Approved	Bitter	Careful
Aggravated	Argumentative	Bored	Careless
Aggressive	Aroused	Bothered	Caring
Agonizing	Assertive	Bound up	Carried away
Agreeable	Astonished	Boxed in	Cautious
Alienated	Attached	Brave	Certain
Alive	Attacked	Breathless	Chased
Alone	Attentive	Bristling	Cheated
Aloof	Attractive	Broken up	Cheerful
Alluring	Aware	Bruised	Choked up
Amazed	Awestruck	Bubbly	Close
Amused	Badgered	Bugged	Cold
Angry	Baited	Burdened	Comfortable
Anguished	Battered	Burned	Comforted
Annoyed	Beaten	Burned up	Competitive

Complacent	Distressed	Grumpy	Lively
Complete	Distrusted	Guarded	Lonely
Confident	Distrustful	Happy-go-lucky	Loose
Conflicted	Dominated	Hard	Lost
Confused	Domineering	Hassled	Loving
Considerate	Doomed	Hateful	Low
Consumed	Double-crossed	Healthy	Lucky
Content	Down	Helpful	Lustful
Cool	Dreadful	Helpless	Mad
Coy	Eager	Hesitant	Malicious
Crabby	Ecstatic	High	Mean
Cranky	Edgy	Hollow	Miserable
Crazy	Elated	Hopeful	Misunderstood
Critical	Embarrassed	Horrified	Moody
Criticized	Empty	Hostile	Mystified
Crushed	Enraged	Humiliated	Nasty
Cuddly	Enraptured	Hung up	Nervous
Curious	Enthusiastic	Hurt	Numb
Cut	Enticed	Hyper	Obsessed
Daring	Esteemed	Ignorant	Offended
Deceived	Exasperated	Impatient	Open
Deceptive	Exhilarated	Important	Ornery
Degraded	Exposed	Impotent	Out of control
Delighted	Fascinated	Impressed	Overjoyed
Demeaned	Flattered	Incompetent	Overwhelmed
Demoralized	Foolish	Incomplete	Pampered
Dependent	Forced	Independent	Panicky
Depressed	Forceful	Innocent	Paralyzed
Deprived	Fortunate	Insecure	Patient
Deserted	Forward	Insignificant	Peaceful
Desirable	Friendly	Insincere	Peeved
Desirous	Frightened	Inspired	Perceptive
Despairing	Frustrated	Insulted	Perturbed
Desperate	Full	Intimate	Petrified
Destroyed	Funny	Intolerant	Phony
Different	Furious	Involved	Pleased
Dirty	Generous	Irate	Powerless
Disappointed	Genuine	Irked	Pressured
Disconnected	Giddy	Irresponsible	Proud
Disgraced	Giving	Irritated	Pulled apart
Disgruntled	Grateful	Jealous	Put down
Disgusted	Greedy	Jittery	Puzzled
Distant	Grim	Joyous	Quarrelsome
Distraught	Grouchy	Left out	Quiet

Raped	Selfish	Submissive	Understanding
Ravished	Separated	Successful	Understood
Ravishing	Shattered	Suffocated	Unfriendly
Real	Shocked	Sure	Unhappy
Refreshed	Shot down	Sweet	Unimportant
Regretful	Shy	Sympathetic	Unimpressed
Rejected	Sickened	Tainted	Unstable
Rejecting	Silly	Tender	Upset
Relaxed	Sincere	Tense	Uptight
Relieved	Sinking	Terrific	Useful
Removed	Smart	Terrified	Valuable
Repulsed	Smothered	Thrilled	Valued
Repulsive	Smug	Ticked	Violated
Resentful	Sneaky	Tickled	Violent
Resistant	Snowed	Tight	Voluptuous
Responsible	Soft	Timid	Vulnerable
Responsive	Soothed	Tired	Warm
Revengeful	Sorry	Tolerant	Weak
Rotten	Spiteful	Tormented	Whipped
Ruined	Spontaneous	Torn	Whole
Safe	Squelched	Tortured	Wild
Satiated	Starved	Trapped	Willing
Satisfied	Stiff	Tremendous	Wiped out
Scared	Stifled	Tricked	Wishful
Scolded	Stimulated	Trustful	Withdrawn
Scorned	Strangled	Ugly	Wonderful
Secure	Strong	Unapproachable	Worried
Seduced	Stubborn	Unaware	Worthy
Seductive	Stunned	Uncertain	Wounded
Self-centered	Stupid	Uncomfortable	Zapped
Self-conscious	Subdued	Under control	

Chapter 13
Victims, Guilt, and Shame

I felt as if I had it written across my forehead: "She was sexual as a child." *I felt as if all people could see into me, could see my secret, and loathed me, as I loathed myself.*

Almost all sexual abuse victims feel guilty about their abuse, as if they were somehow responsible for it. Almost all victims struggle with some measure of self-loathing or self-hatred. Almost all victims feel shame, as if the world would reject them if it knew about their abuse. This chapter will provide suggestions as to how to overcome the feelings of guilt and shame.

REAL AND FALSE GUILT

There are two types of guilt: real and false.
Real guilt is a fact. Whether one feels guilty or not is irrelevant.

Indeed, many people are factually guilty but don't feel guilty. Perpetrators fall into this category.

There are four types of real guilt. When one breaks the Ten Commandments or any other biblical commands, he is guilty of breaking *God's laws*. When one drives her car over the speed limit or robs a store, she is guilty of breaking *the law*. When one burps loudly at a social function or reveals secrets that are embarrassing to others, he is guilty of breaking *unwritten social standards*. When one tells the world that she is on a diet but sneaks pie and ice cream, she is guilty of breaking *personal standards*. Real guilt involves genuine responsibility for guilt.

False guilt is a feeling of guilt when one is not factually guilty— when she has no responsibility for wrongdoing. For example, if Sally is standing nearby when Connie steals a cookie, and their mother scolds both girls for stealing cookies, Sally may feel guilty even though it was Connie who stole the cookie. Sexual abuse victims are usually masters at assuming guilt even though they are not guilty. And perpetrators usually work very diligently to deny their own guilt and heap the guilt onto their victims: "She seduced me." "I couldn't help myself."

The Victim's Dilemma

Almost all victims feel guilty. The reason usually is that the victim was present when the abuse happened. Most victims mentally chastise themselves with "should" messages: "You should have stopped the abuse." "You should have been smarter." "You should not have let it happen to you." "You should have gone for help." "You should have resisted." "You should have run away." "You should not have been so stupid." "You should have known!" These messages only serve to increase the level of false guilt that the victim already feels.

False Guilt and Self-Hatred

False guilt combined with these heavy "should" messages are the predominant reasons why many victims continue to hate themselves. They feel responsible for their abuse, that it was somehow their fault. They loathe what happened to them, and they adopt all of it as their personal responsibility to carry for the rest of their lives. "Everything was my fault!" is a common feeling expressed by victims. However, here is a fact: No matter what happened, your abuse was not your fault. You are not guilty of anything.

The next section does not intend to imply that victims enjoy their abuse. Rather, it is intended to deal with a struggle that many victims express. Are they guilty of their own abuse because they felt sexually stimulated during the abuse or because they may have repeatedly gone back to their abuser?

False Guilt and Sexual Stimulation

Sexual abuse, although a terribly wrong thing for a perpetrator to do, can in some circumstances feel stimulating to a victim. Some victims are seriously confused because they felt sexually stimulated while they were being fondled or raped. This is not to say that these victims enjoyed the abuse. They may have felt sexually stimulated because their bodies were healthy and experienced pleasure when touched in certain ways. This can result in profound confusion and anxiety for the victim.

If the perpetrator was gentle and manipulative, the sexual experience might have even been somewhat pleasant, even while it was confusing and disturbing. This is absolutely not to say that the victim invited the abuse.

Further compounding the problem, some victims are put into a position of power over others in the family system. For example, if a father is abusing his daughter and also gives the daughter his authority to make family decisions—thereby placing the girl in power over the mother—then the sexual abuse may somehow appear to be appropriate (at the moment). Some fathers who are abusers tell their daughters that Mother is sexually incompetent. That's the reason given why Dad turns to Daughter for sexual companionship.

In this type of circumstance the daughter may feel her body being turned on and may even occasionally initiate sexual activity. When she reaches adulthood, she can find it terribly difficult to process her guilt feelings. Many victims feel that they are sick or abnormal because during the abuse their body did what it was supposed to do. But let's use reason for a moment. Pinch the nose hard enough and it will bleed. Kick the shins and they'll bruise. Engage in sexual activity and one is likely to feel stimulated and may even reach orgasm. The fact that one's body reacts in a normal way doesn't mean that the victim asked for the abuse. Nor does it mean that she is sick or abnormal.

Let's keep this in perspective: adults are adults, and children are children. For an adult to sexually use a child is not only morally wrong; it is illegal. Even if the child is relationally or emotionally manipulated to the point that she pursues the abuser toward the objective of sexual stimulation, it is still the adult who is morally and legally culpable. Period.

Some victims live with awful doubts. "Was I sexually curious?" "Did I enjoy the sense of closeness or learning about sexual activity?" "Did I encourage it?" "Why didn't I try to stop it?" "Were there needs I had that were being met?"

In some cases the answer to each of these questions may be a partial yes. Even so, the adult is still morally and legally culpable. There is a place for normal childhood sexual curiosity. There is a place for enjoyment of normal physical closeness. Some victims are manipulated to the point of not wishing to stop the sexual activity, and we could list a host of needs that are partially addressed by sexual activity. But none of these facts takes the perpetrator off the hook. None of them places the burden of guilt on the victim.

Even if the girl has some feelings of curiosity, even if she feels sexually aroused, the adult abuser must be held morally responsible. If this is not obvious to you, you are still thinking as a victim.

False guilt is a powerful thing. It makes victims feel guilty for crimes committed by perpetrators. Victims of sexual abuse are no more guilty than are victims of mugging. Let's explore how you can shed the false guilt.

HOW TO PROCESS GUILT

Following are several steps you can take to help yourself move beyond the guilt feelings associated with your abuse. Be diligent and thorough in journaling your answers.

1. *Be specific about what you feel.* There it is again, that word *specific.* Write down what you feel, of what you might be guilty.

Name it. This is a very important exercise; without it the next several exercises will be useless. Take some time. Write several pages.

2. *Distinguish between real and false guilt.* Separate facts from feelings. Are you struggling with actions of adult, informed intent that you took in order to be sexually abused? Or are you dealing with feelings of being stained and wretched? If the latter, then you are probably dealing primarily with false guilt. Everyone knows that you can't stand next to a skunk without coming away smelling like a skunk. But that doesn't mean you *are* a skunk! So go back to what you wrote in answering question 1. As you identify issues of real or true guilt, in red ink write a big letter *T*. For issues of false guilt or guilt feelings, write a big red letter *F*.

3. *Choose to let go of all the F's.* You now have a pretty good list of the false guilt items that probably drive you crazy. None of those F's are your fault! You must now intentionally, vigorously, *and with anger* decide not to allow yourself to believe any of those false guilt messages any longer—for the rest of your life. This is an appropriate use of your anger. You have been lied to! Use your anger to protect yourself from further victimizing yourself.

Victims are often adept at holding onto feelings of guilt and responsibility for all sorts of things for which they factually carry no responsibility. This is a message that often permeates a victim's entire life. She frequently becomes an overresponsible person, taking on the sins of the world as her personal mission. So stop it. Work on identifying where your responsibility ends and the rest of the world's responsibility begins.

Mentally put all of the guilt and guilt feelings, whether true or false, into a garbage can and dump them into a garbage truck. Watch the garbage truck drive away, never to return. If you're a Christian, take the load of guilt and guilt feelings to the cross and leave it there. That's where it belongs anyway.

You may have to release your guilt feelings many times. That's OK. Do so as often as you need until they are all gone.

4. *Allow yourself the helplessness and/or mistakes of a child.* Many victims weep when asked if they would be as hard on their own daughters as they are on themselves. Their answer is almost always, "No! I would never be this hard on my daughter. I would love her, hold her, and let her feel my arms around her while she cries."

Try doing this victim's exercise. Go to a safe place. Get comfortable. Close your eyes. Relax. Breathe deeply. Imagine yourself as you were when you were a child. Look at yourself for a while. Then, as the adult you are now, reach out your hand to the child that you were. Ask that little girl to come to you. Ask her if you may just hug her for a little while.

As you hold her in your arms, tell her that you forgive her for everything, whether real or imagined. Then ask her to forgive you for being so harsh with her as a result of what happened to her. Forgive and ask for forgiveness. Cry as much as you wish. Both you and your "little girl" have every right to a good cry.

5. *Forgive yourself for anything for which you were truly responsible.* We all make mistakes. Sometimes they're little mistakes, and sometimes they're big ones. But mentally whipping yourself for something that happened years ago does absolutely no good.

If you are a spiritual person, then you *must* forgive yourself. The Bible says that we are to love our neighbor as ourselves (see Mark 12:33). If you don't love yourself, then you can't love anyone else. You can only use others and be used by them.

Self-love is axiomatic to mental health and interpersonal relationships. If you wish to experience genuine love, you must begin with genuine self-acceptance. You'll actually damage all your relationships until you are able to accept yourself as lovable and capable.

Suppose that you marry and your husband tells you that he loves you. If you hate yourself, mentally you can only give him three options: (a) he's lying; (b) he has deluded himself; (c) he's kind but ignorant, and when he really comes to his senses or learns the truth he'll hate you too. This is a trap that victims build for themselves. The bottom line is: you must forgive yourself.

6. *Set a specific date by which you will stop punishing yourself.* How long will you hate the little girl who was abused? How long will you hate the adult she has become? How long will you loathe yourself? You can and must stop. Pick a date and circle it on your calendar. On that date declare a personal war against all self-debasing, self-loathing, self-criticizing, self-destructive, self-hating activities and thoughts. You may not be able to stop thoughts from entering your head, but you must stop feeding and nurturing them. Work at replacing them with kindness, gentleness, forgiveness, happiness, encouragement, patience, and health.

If you find it difficult or impossible to stop punishing yourself, at least take a half step. Limit your self-punishment from (for example) 7:00–8:00 A.M., three days a week. If you wish to punish yourself at any other time, tell yourself that you have to wait until Friday morning at 7:00 A.M. Actually, this could play to one of your strengths, because survivors of abuse are often masters at putting things off.

7. *Ask for God's forgiveness and healing.* God is far more willing to forgive and love you than you are to forgive yourself. God can handle our mistakes. We condemn ourselves for our mistakes more than anyone else could ever do. The entire focus of the Bible is God's ability to accept, forgive, cleanse, heal, and empower people even through the worst of circumstances.

GUILT AND SELF-ESTEEM

Once upon a time there was a pretty little girl. She lived in the country and loved to go for long walks in the open fields. She always wore a pretty white dress and loved to stop and pick wildflowers. She had lovely, long golden hair.

One day while she was picking wildflowers an evil man came upon her and carried her off through the woods. He dragged her through thorny bushes and a stinky swamp. He tore her pretty white dress. Her face and arms were cut badly, but he didn't care. Her beautiful hair was disheveled and torn. He took her to his dirty cave and abused her.

Terrified, weeping, she was finally able to break away from him, running blindly, wildly. Although her cuts stopped bleeding and the bloodstains dried, she kept running. She ran until the moisture from the swamp and mud had dried. She was free of him, but her dress was torn and filthy, her face and arms were badly cut, and her hair was matted with mud and twigs.

The next day she found a cape and wrapped it tightly around herself to hide the mud, bloodstains, and scars. She used the cape's hood to cover most of her face. She never removed the cape; to do so would have meant exposing the filth and the wounds.

Years passed. One day she met a mystic who could mend her dress, cleanse it pure white again, and erase the scars from her arms and face. She asked for help and was given all she asked for. Yet she found the change difficult to accept, for she had lived long with the torn dress, mud, dried blood, scars, and protective cape.

She found that her soul was more scarred than her arms and face had been. Her spirit was more torn and muddied than her dress. As she walked away from the mystic he called after her, "You must now let go of the cape, for it will only remind you of the past. You must now smile at the sun, or you will forever fear the darkness of the cave. You must now comb your hair and wash your face, or you will forever think of yourself as being ugly."

Torn, stained, and bruised self-esteem is perhaps the most constant and pervasive symptom of sexual abuse. False guilt feelings are the logs that fuel the fire of low self-esteem. Your perpetrator used the axe of sin to cut the logs of guilt, then heaped them upon the fire of your self-abasement. You must stop adding his fuel to the fire that burns your self-esteem. His hand lit the match. Your hand must pour on the water of forgiveness, self-love, and kindness.

Guilt, Self-Esteem, and Sex

Victims often have problems with sexually intimate relationships. Low self-esteem is a primary factor in this dilemma, and much of low self-esteem is driven by false guilt. If you are a married victim struggling with enjoyment of sexuality, read the following self-messages that may be helpful as you consider lovemaking.

- I was a child then. I'm an adult now.
- I was being manipulated or forced then, but now I want to learn to enjoy my sexuality without fear.
- Abuse is ugly and embarrassing, but sex with my husband is enjoyable.
- It was not OK to be sexual then. It is OK now.
- Sex was dangerous and humiliating then. Now it is to be enjoyed and appreciated.
- My abuser was evil. My husband is very different from my abuser.
- I was powerless then. Now I can say no. I have rights!
- I felt guilty then. Now I can make love and still be pure.

• It used to be dangerous for me to be me. Now it is good for me to be me, and I choose to be who I am.

Following are a few more then-and-now statements to help you practice this separation.

• *Then* I used to feel_____, but
  now I am free to feel_____.

• *Then* I used to think_____, but
  now I am free to think_____.

• *Then* I used to be afraid because_____
  _____, but *now* I don't need to be afraid because
  _____.

• *Then* I used to think of my body as_____
  _____, but
  now I can think of my body as_____
  _____.

• *Then* I used to act_____, but
  now I am free to act_____.

• *Then* my guilt used to_____
  _____, but
  now I am determined to_____
  _____.

Your abuser piled false guilt on your shoulders. How long will you carry it? When will you choose to use your anger to remove his guilt from your shoulders? How long will you choose to carry that which belongs to him? How long will you punish yourself on his account?

What would it mean for you to release your guilt feelings? To whom would you release them? How would you go about doing so? If the feelings returned, could you release them again? And again? What would it feel like to have real peace in your life?

GUILT VERSUS SHAME

Guilt, a personal matter, is what we feel or know about *ourselves*. Shame is how we feel about our guilt or guilt feelings as related to a significant person in our lives. For example, when I was a child I tried to steal a candy bar from a local grocery store. I was caught. In stealing the candy bar I was *factually guilty*. When I got caught I *felt guilty*. But when the store owner called my father and told him, I experienced *shame*.

Victims often fear public exposure of their presumed guilt, leading to shame. More often than not, victims who fear shame grew up in what may be called *shame-bound systems*. Shame has often been used as a motivator or a deterrent. "Shame on you" is a phrase often used by parents.

The shame-bound system within which some victims grow up is as much a culprit as is the perpetrator himself. Such a system creates the idea that if the child doesn't live up to a certain level of expectation, she will be rejected. Shame-bound families can't handle truth.

The shame-bound system is seen in the mother who denies reality by saying, "My little girl would never do something as filthy as that!" It's seen in the brothers who molest their sister and then say, "They'll think you're no good if they find out." It's seen in the abuser who says, "If you tell about this I'll tell the whole world that you asked for this." It's seen in the high-school teacher who fondles a girl and then threatens to ruin her reputation if she says anything publicly.

Shame Follows a Breach of Personal Boundaries

Shame-bound systems are usually characterized by rules that demand and enforce control, blame, perfectionism, and denial of reality. Shame-bound systems typically enforce three cardinal rules: don't think, don't talk, and don't feel. Fossum and Mason define shame: "Shame results when a person's body, thoughts, or feelings are invaded in such a way that the person feels like, and is subsequently treated like, an object or a thing."[1]

Shame follows when personal boundaries have been breached. Shame usually results in the creation of walls to protect against anyone knowing of this boundary breachment. Boundaries seem to be one's friends; walls may provide protection, but they are usually not healthy.

How to Overcome Shame

Overcoming shame involves one simple task. Tell the truth openly, and let the chips fall where they may. Carrying shame around in one's heart is like carrying a dead fish in one's purse. One can't allow herself to get too close to others or they'll smell the fish. Getting the fish out of the purse is part of the healing process.

Healing involves cleaning out shame, opening windows and doors, telling the truth, and being completely honest. It means being once again able to trust, to feel, to talk openly, to laugh freely, and to relate closely. But first the fish must be removed from the purse.

You might be worrying about what impact your telling the truth may have on your abuser. In the final analysis it will do one thing: invite him to face the truth too.

QUESTIONS FOR REFLECTION

1. Do you feel guilty about your abuse? If so, why? Be specific.

2. Is your guilt true or false guilt? Tie your answers to specific situations, experiences, memories, and so on.

3. Why is it so difficult for the little girl in the story to take off the cape? What parts of your life are similar to the cape she wore?

4. How does your guilt keep you from feeling pure, clean, whole, and free?

5. How did your abuser set you up to transfer his guilt feelings to you?

6. How are your guilt feelings tied to shame? Who should be feeling shamed? In what important relationships do you feel shame?

7. Suppose your abuse became known publicly, and everyone said you were not at fault. What effect would this have on your ability to feel peaceful, pure, and whole?

=== *ACTION ITEMS* ===

Write down five examples from the past week in which you have felt guilty or shamed in any way (for example, at home with your kids, in the office, in relating to your husband, or on a date). Then reflect upon the following statements.

Abused women frequently feel guilty about almost everything in the world. If you're like this, do some thinking. Why are you so quick to feel guilt or shame? How are your present feelings of guilt or shame tied to similar feelings in the past? Answer this question in writing.

Abused women also frequently turn other emotions (anger, fear, sadness, even joy) into feelings of guilt or shame. If you do this, ask yourself why. How did you learn to do this? How can you change? Do you *want* to change? Reflectively, write your answers.

FOR SPIRITUAL GROWTH

Read and reflect upon the following Scripture passages, and write down one thing that you can learn from each one: Psalm 51:1–14; Isaiah 1:18; Ezekiel 18:20–32 (if you feel that you were somehow responsible for your abuse); Matthew 11:28–30; Titus 1:15 (especially as it applies to your abuser); Hebrews 10:22; 1 Peter 5:7.

Chapter 14
Processing Guilt

In this chapter we'll focus on steps of processing guilt. Consider these steps as skills to be mastered. Face the truth. Repent. Confess your guilt. Accept God's forgiveness. Forgive yourself. Ask forgiveness of those you've wronged. Choose health and honesty. And be as constructive as you can in making amends.

FACE THE TRUTH

There are many ways in which people attempt to avoid facing the truth of their own guilt. Some use denial, repression, or suppression. Others are into blaming. Some compare themselves with others and then feel either horrible or slightly vindicated. Most use some form of rationalization. Many attempt to overcompensate in some area of their lives, as if to say, "I'm not guilty of *that* because I am so good at doing *this*." To rid oneself of guilt, one must face the truth.

REPENT

To repent means to entirely stop the wrong that one is doing. The ancient Greeks used the word to imply a 180-degree turn—for example, from going north to going south. Repentance involves a sense of being sorry for wrongs done and implies a change of heart.

One can't repent of that which one refuses to admit as being real. That's why the first step in processing guilt requires honesty and facing the truth. Even if you're struggling with false guilt and need to unload it, all of these skills will apply.

CONFESS YOUR GUILT

Confession is a magnificently healing practice. Perhaps one story from my life will illustrate. In my midlife I am beginning to recognize that I have been a pretty demanding father.

I am fortunate to have a wife who is able to share these kinds of observations with me; and I am finally maturing enough to hear what she has to say. One evening my wife and I had been discussing this issue when our oldest daughter, Gretchen, came home from a date. I called Gretchen into our bedroom and said, "Gretchen, I am beginning to realize that I have been a pretty demanding daddy, and I have pushed you too hard lots of times. Without ever intending to do so I have hurt you. I love you with all my heart, Gretchen, and I am really sorry for being so tough on you. Would you forgive me? I'm going to work real hard on being a better dad for you."

Gretchen's eyes welled up with tears. She murmured, "Sure, I forgive you," gave me a big hug, and then rushed off to her room to have a good cry. She knew I'd been too demanding for many years. The only person in our family who didn't know was me. When I realized this truth about myself I had to repent and then confess to those whom I had hurt.

Since that point of repentance and confession, my relationship with Gretchen has healed. Today we are as close as I can imagine any father and daughter. Guilt can be processed. Healing does happen.

ACCEPT GOD'S FORGIVENESS; FORGIVE YOURSELF; ASK FORGIVENESS OF OTHERS

Clean the slates—no hidden agendas, nothing left unforgiven. And then live your life by the truth. Stop the self-abasement. Stop reinforcing messages of failure. The hardest part of this task will probably be self-forgiveness.

CHOOSE HEALTH AND HONESTY

To continue to carry grudges, whether against oneself, God, or others, will continually lead to dysfunctional and counterproductive relationships and low self-esteem. Healing from guilt requires choosing what is healthy (positive, constructive, healing, nurturing) and what is honest.

You can choose to continue in the swamp of your abuse. Or you can choose to bathe in God's love and forgiveness and be clean.

MAKE AMENDS AS YOU ARE ABLE

Begin with yourself. If you are factually guilty of something, it can be helpful and healing to at least attempt to make amends.

Some victims attempt to drastically overcompensate in making amends. In this case the overcompensation becomes the central theme in the relationship. The message is, "If I can heap immense gifts upon the person I've wronged, maybe I can give more than I took away, and then the score will be evened."

Making amends is not done to even a score but to demonstrate one's sincerity in repentance. The best form of making amends is a truly changed life.

BE CONSTRUCTIVE IN PROCESSING YOUR OWN GUILT

Bruce Narramore uses a paradigm to help people understand how to process guilt. It compares unconstructive and constructive guilt management. He calls unconstructive guilt management "psychological guilt" and constructive guilt management "constructive sorrow."[1]

	Psychological Guilt	Constructive Sorrow
Person in primary focus:	Yourself	God or others
Attitudes or actions in primary focus:	Past misdeeds	Damage done to others or our future correct deeds
Motivation for change (if any):	To avoid feeling bad (guilt feelings)	To help others, to promote our growth, to do God's will (love feelings)
Attitude toward oneself:	Anger and frustration	Love and respect, combined with concern
Result:	(a) External change (for improper motivations) (b) Stagnation due to paralyzing effect of guilt (c) Rebellion	Repentance and change based on an attitude of love and mutual respect

LEARN TO USE SPIRITUALITY

In many victims' lives religion has been used punitively. There-fore, it will be important for you to distinguish between *religion* and *spirituality*. Religion per se can sometimes be an awful burden as one attempts to process guilt. On the other hand, true spiritu-ality, true contact with God, is a freeing experience. Picture yourself walking to the cross of Christ with an immense burden on your back. It is the burden of your guilt. Picture yourself unstrapping the burden and laying it at the foot of the cross. Then picture yourself walking away from the cross with no burden of guilt.

DON'T ACCEPT FAILURE AS THE FINAL WORD

There's not a person who has not failed in some way. Some failures affect others' lives and some do not. Victims often tend to think they have committed an unforgivable sin or that they are irremediably stained. This type of thinking tends only to further spread the sense of failure and worthlessness. If you are factually guilty of anything, you now know how to process your guilt.

Avoid the mistake of feeling that failure is the last word in your life. You can be free of your guilt. You can once again pursue and enjoy life to its fullest.

QUESTIONS FOR REFLECTION

1. Of what do you need to confess and repent? Name several events or attitudes. Be specific.

2. Do you carry true or false guilt about these events or attitudes?

3. What life beliefs do you carry as a result of your abuse? How can you use what you learned in this chapter to help you grow beyond some of these beliefs?

4. If you were God, would you have created guilt? What purpose does it serve?

5. At what point does guilt become counterproductive to the purposes for which God intended it?

6. From reading the steps in this chapter, what do you see as the hardest part of processing guilt?

ACTION ITEMS

1. Name one matter about which you are struggling with true guilt feelings._____

_____

_____

_____

2. Write a prayer of repentance._____

_____

_____

_____

_____.

3. This week tell one person that you are repenting of (name the situation).

4. As if you were God, write a note to yourself. Tell yourself that God forgives you._____

_____

_____

_____

_____

_____.

5. Write a note to yourself, this time from yourself. Say that you forgive yourself, and sign your note._____

_____

_____

_____

_____.

_____
Signed

6. If you need to ask forgiveness of another person, do so this week. List the names of those of whom you need to ask forgiveness.

1. _____   3. _____

2. _____   4. _____

7. Write a statement about what it will mean in your life to choose health for yourself from now on._____

_____

_____

_____.

8. List amends that you could make in order to demonstrate your sincerity.

Person: Amends I could undertake:

_____   _____

                                 _____

                                 _____

_____   _____

                                 _____

                                 _____

FOR SPIRITUAL GROWTH

1. Memorize Isaiah 43:25 and Jeremiah 31:34*b*.

2. Read 2 Chronicles 7:14. What does this verse say about God's willingness to forgive even an entire nation? What steps are required for forgiveness?

3. King David made some big mistakes in his life. His prayer of repentance is found in Psalm 51.

4. Read Psalm 65:3. What does this say about what God does with our transgressions?

5. Read Proverbs 3:7–8. What does this passage say about the effects of turning away from evil?

6. Read Jeremiah 3:12–13. Again, what does God want from us when we have made mistakes?

7. Ezekiel 18:20–32 carries the same theme and covers it more thoroughly. Read this passage.

Chapter 15
No Longer Victims of Fear

When I was in college, one of my roommates had just returned from Vietnam. He had been in several battles. Consequently, when he returned to the United States he was edgy. During the first few days as he was walking around, a dog would bark or a twig would snap. He would instinctively leap behind a nearby garage or dive to the ground behind a tree or fence. His war memories stayed with him. Sometimes at night he would wake up in a cold sweat, reliving a firefight and hearing men scream. It was some time before he could resume normal living.

This chapter deals with processing fear. Women who have been sexually abused frequently carry deep fears. Fear is normal and valuable. Fear can be a friend. It can keep a person from dangerous situations and mobilize a person to flee when danger approaches.

Normal fear evokes many physical responses. The heart rate

increases; one's senses become more acute; one may gain greater physical strength as adrenaline is pumped into the bloodstream. The body prepares for "fight or flight."

Fear can also be an enemy, wearing down a person, robbing her of health, and keeping her from enjoying positive relationships. Fear associated with sexual abuse frequently robs victims of the normal ability to enjoy a free-flowing relationship with husbands, friends, and family. One victim sometimes wakes up in the middle of the night in a cold sweat, with a recurring dream that is based in her abuse. Some victims do not want to date for fear of having to deal with their sexuality.

FEAR AND ONGOING BELIEF SYSTEMS

To sustain a long-term fear, one must carry an ongoing belief system regarding the fear-evoking source. She must believe that there continues to be some danger associated with the fear-evoking source. This belief system may be conscious or unconscious. It can be illustrated by the experience of falling off a horse. If one does not immediately remount the horse, he may fear horses for the rest of his life.

When a girl is sexually abused, she may experience deep fear either during or after the abuse. Those feelings of fear may be conscious, or they may be so overwhelming that she pushes them into her unconscious. She may know exactly of what she is afraid; or she may have vague memories that seem to keep her away from or drive her toward certain people, activities, or places.

SPECIFIC FEAR CAN BECOME GENERALIZED FEAR

Unresolved fear of specific issues can sometimes become generalized fear. Following are some examples of unresolved fear messages that have become generalized fear messages in the life of a victim.

"Men are dangerous. They'll all use and abuse you."

"Sex is dangerous. You'll feel terrible if you make love, even with someone you love."

"Women are dangerous. They'll abandon you, even when you're hurting."

"Relationships are dangerous. They'll eventually hurt you."

"Sharing your pain is dangerous. If you ever do, people will reject you."

To overcome fear, one must be willing to challenge her belief systems. Fear is usually rational *at its source*. If you are driving a car on a two-lane highway and see an oncoming car passing another, coming right at you with a closing speed of 120 miles per hour, it's rational to feel fear. If you refuse to ride in a car forever because of the fear you experienced on that highway, your fear becomes less rational. Left unresolved, fear often generalizes.

Fortunately, as we age we are more able to use our cognitive adult selves to "talk to" the frightened little person inside us. It is possible for most adults to use their advanced knowledge and skills to overcome their fears. However this is not an easy task for a deeply traumatized person to accomplish. The fear-evoking source remains too powerful, often at an unconscious level.

Following is a short exercise to help you process some of the generalizations that you may have. Finish the sentences, using your best adult, cognitive self.

My abuser was a jerk, but all men in general_____

_____.

Sexual abuse is an awful experience, but making love with some-one I love and am married to might be_____

_____.

My mother didn't rescue me from my abuser, but women in general_____

_____.

It may be frightening to share the story of my abuse with another person. But some people will love me even if I tell them all about it, and_____

_____.

When a person has irrational fear, she is usually associating it with some other experience. With courage and commitment to oneself, it is possible for a victim to challenge and overcome her fears. A person is not usually able to do this alone. By sharing with other women and experiencing their support, a victim can best work at overcoming her fears.

FEAR AND PROMISCUITY

Almost anyone can understand the association between abuse and fear of sexuality. But how is it possible for an abuse victim to become promiscuous? Aren't the two experiences mutually exclusive?

Reaction Formation

The answer may be as simple as understanding the power of psychological defense mechanisms frequently used by people who are terrified. One such defense is called *reaction formation*.

During her first years in social work, a psychologist had been assigned to work in the projects—apartment buildings for the poor. These projects had a reputation for being extremely dangerous. There were frequent rapes, murders, robberies, assaults, and so on.

Yet she was not afraid. She walked freely through the projects, stepping over drunks and even riding the elevators! Then one day she realized that she was actually so terrified that she had repressed her fears and had replaced them with feelings of bravery. That's an example of *reaction formation*.

Some victims use this defense mechanism to prove to themselves that they're not really wounded, that they're not afraid of their sexuality, and that they are in control of their lives. When they go from one sexual partner to another they act out the message, "I'm not anyone's victim! I'm not afraid of sex. I'm in control."

Fear of Loss of Affection

Another way in which fear can drive a woman to promiscuity is through an internal message that says, "You are not lovable." Fear of being unlovable or of living without being loved can be a powerful driver. Many victims report feeling more or less worthless unless in the arms of a lover.

Fear of Loss of Self

Yet other victims report a fear of losing their very identity, their core, unless they are sexually active. Many of these victims were

told that they were useless for anything but sex. Therefore they fear
that if they're not sexual, they're nothing.

COMMON EFFECTS OF FEAR

Relational Isolation

Victims often live in relational isolation (even within marriage)
and choose friends or husbands who will not get "too close."

"What if they found out?" "What would they think of me?"
"How could they ever accept me if they knew?" These kinds of
fears, coupled with the suspicion that if anyone does find out they'll
quickly leave the relationship, keep many victims disconnected
from nurturing and meaningful relationships. This can occur even
within marriage, as victims find mates who are themselves unable
or unwilling to enter into deep intimacy.

Continued Low Self-Esteem

It's almost impossible to live with constant fear and feel good
about oneself. Ongoing fear keeps one a victim. When one
constantly fears recurrence of the abuse or public discovery of her
secret, she will live somewhat at arm's length from caring relationships. Therefore she will continue to be a victim.

Physical Symptoms

Any time the body is kept in a constant state of readiness for
fight or flight, physical symptoms will occur. (The major physical
symptoms were listed in chapter 11.) To live in a state of fear does
physical damage to one's body.

Complications of Fear

Unresolved fear often invites other friends to the party. Fear's
eager friends are anxiety, guilt, and anger. Anxiety is a free-floating
sense that you are about to step on a banana peel, fall, and break
your back. The association between guilt and fear will be explored
later in this chapter. The sense that you can't get away from the fear

that keeps you a victim should make you angry, as should living with a general sense of helplessness because of fear. Failing to deal with fear often opens the door to other friends coming to the victim party.

PROCESSING FEAR

Name Your Fears—Be Specific

In this book you have repeatedly been asked to be specific in naming your emotions. It's not enough to simply say, "I'm afraid." Specifically, of what are you afraid? Following are some examples of specific fears issuing from general fears.

Unspecific	*Specific*
"I'm afraid of sex."	"I'm afraid that if I feel sexual stimulation again, I'll emotionally relive all the horrors and humiliation of my abuse."
"I'm afraid of men."	"I'm afraid that all men in the entire world are out of control and that, if given the chance, they will rape me."
"I'm afraid of getting too close to people."	"I'm afraid that if I get close to another person, he will find out about my abuse and then reject or humiliate me."
"I'm afraid of remembering too much."	"I'm afraid that if I allow my memories to exist, they will tell me that I was seductive or that I wanted the abuse. I'm also afraid that if I remember too much, I'll find out that my abuse was worse than I think it was."
"I think women are jerks."	"I needed my mother to help me when I was being abused, and she didn't. Now I struggle with women as friends."

The more specific you can be regarding your fears, the more you will find that you have created your own healing path.

Associate Present Fears and Past Experiences

It may sound simple, but this exercise is one of the core tools used in psychoanalysis. A simple way to frame this exercise is by using the following sentence: "I am afraid of_____ because when I was being abused I felt_____."

As you make these associations, don't think that you are some-how locked in to live in certain ways due to your abuse. You have just as much right, power, and motivation to experience life in the manner *you choose* as do all of those "normal" women. (Most victims seem to assume that women who weren't sexually abused are nor-mal, and they, the victims, are not.)

Assert Your Own Strength

Some victims seem to hide in a dark corner, hoping never to be seen. They speak quietly and never say or do anything that would make another person upset. When asked, "Where is your anger?" such a woman will frequently say, "It's not ladylike to be angry." That is a variation on the theme that women are allowed to be sad or fearful, but they're not supposed to be angry. That's what many victims learn, and they learn the lesson well: Don't assert your own strength. Don't fight back. Don't be angry. Don't accept your own emotions. Don't think; don't feel; don't act. Just wait until it's over.

To heal, one of the fears you will have to face is that of accepting your feelings and asserting yourself. And to heck with what every-one else thinks about it! Sure, you might overdo some of your self-assertion, at least at the beginning, but that's OK. The only way you can learn to properly assess and manage your strength is to exercise it.

Stop Running from the Dogs

If you've ever run away from a threatening dog, you've probably been bitten. Dogs tend to nip at those who run from them. But most dogs can be faced down and overcome with words such as "No! Down! Bad! Go home! Stop!"

Sexual abuse often teaches victims to run from everything. The abuse makes them feel helpless and hopeless. To build a lifetime of running, however, will have the effect of being bitten many times. It's better to face the dogs than to run away from them.

Take a moment and name some of your most fearsome "dogs":

_____

_____

_____

_____

_____

Constant running reinforces a sense of helplessness and erodes one's self-confidence and self-respect. Is that what you want?

Stop All Victim Self-Talk

Following are some examples of common victim self-talk. Consider how each one keeps the woman tied up in her fears.

"I'm stained forever."

"I'll never be normal."

"I've ruined my whole life."

"I can't be open with anyone."

"I'm not strong enough to stand up to anyone."

"I'm just a dumb, gullible person."

Victims keep themselves victims by talking to themselves like victims.

Change Your Expectations

You might not believe the forthcoming statement to be true; after all, you didn't enter life expecting to be abused, and there are exceptions to the rule. But generally the principle is true: people tend to both see and experience that which they expect. Perhaps a story might help you see the point.

A king wanted to find out whether his kingdom contained more weeds or more flowers. He called two men into his court. To the first he gave the assignment of cataloging all the weeds in his kingdom. The second man was given the assignment of cataloging all the flowers. They were given two months to complete their assignments.

At the end of two months they returned to the king. The first said, "O mighty king, your kingdom is covered in weeds! It's a horrible sight! You must do something about it! It's sad to have so many weeds overrunning your kingdom."

The second man said, "O mighty king, your kingdom is absolutely overrun with flowers of every kind and color. They are glorious. They make your kingdom fresh and alive. It is a joy to be part of your kingdom."

What we *expect* to see colors what we *do* see in life. In dealing with fear, changing your expectations is part of the healing process. You were hurt once, perhaps many times; but there are flowers in the kingdom if you wish to find them. Your life is not ruined because of weeds unless you decide to quit on yourself. When you do this, your abuser wins again.

Focus on the Present

Fear is frequently tied to the past. Look at the present for what it is. Not all male/female relationships are painful. Not all women are helpless. Today and tomorrow have no writing upon them yet.

Set Goals; Take One Step at a Time

A therapist told of a client who had been in a hotel in which a large gallery had collapsed, killing several people. The client wanted to be able to go back into the hotel, but had a deathly fear of doing so.

My friend used a therapeutic technique called *desensitization*, which involved taking the client closer and closer, one day at a time, to the scene. At first they drove within a few blocks of the hotel. On another day they drove within visual sight of it. Then they drove past it. Then they walked past it; then they walked into the lobby. They finally had lunch in the hotel dining room.

In overcoming fear it can be helpful to set goals and then work toward them, one small step at a time. Each step might be scary, but that's OK. Break your big goals down into small steps. Then take the steps. Keep taking steps every day.

A friend of mine has lived life with the motto: "Do one scary thing every day." This person is a delight to be around at age eighty! Big goals sometimes require small steps. Keep pushing your edges further and further. Don't stop. Don't quit on yourself.

QUESTIONS FOR REFLECTION

1. What are three or four of your most common fears? Write them down on paper, and consider how they may be associated with your abuse.

2. Has your life-style become one of fear? If so, how? Write three or four paragraphs about this.

3. Reflect upon how powerlessness and fear are connected. In what ways might you begin to take control of your life? What would it feel like for you to have power? In what way would you use your power? What feelings would come under your control if you had power?

4. How can fear keep a victim in the cycle of helplessness and interpersonal isolation?

5. How can anger be an ally as you take steps toward overcoming your fears? Are there other sources of strength that you may tap? Can you think of four?

═══ ACTION ITEMS ═══

1. Complete the following:

Fears I have:	How these fears are tied to my abuse:	Sources of power I can tap to overcome these fears:
a.	a.	a.
b.	b.	b.
c.	c.	c.

d.	d.	d.
e.	e.	e.
f.	f.	f.

2. Identify three areas in which you feel stuck in dealing with your fears. These may concern relationships, work, your spouse, children, parents, or personal accomplishments. Write down what you would like to accomplish if you could—one goal for each area in which you're stuck.

Areas where I'm stuck:	*Goals for overcoming:*
a.	a.
b.	b.
c.	c.

FOR SPIRITUAL GROWTH

1. Read Psalm 23. What do you think David meant by the "valley of the shadow of death"? Was it death itself, some deep fear, or sadness? How did he make the decision to walk through the valley? Did he walk through it alone? Even though David obviously believed in the constant presence of God, do you think that David still felt alone?

2. The rod and staff mentioned in this psalm were shepherds' tools. The staff was a long stick with a crook or loop at the end, used for pulling sheep out of crevasses. The rod was used to stave off predators. Which of these two shepherds' tools would you most wish for God to use, and how would you wish for God to use it?

3. The shepherd always walked at the head of his flock. In this way he always faced the dangers of the trail first, before the sheep. What does this image conjure in your mind as you consider your healing process?

4. Read 1 John 4:18. What does this verse mean? How is love (both being loved and loving oneself) tied to defeating fear? In your own life, identify areas in which you (a) do not feel loved and (b) do not love yourself. How do these empty emotional areas perpetuate your feelings of fear?

Chapter 16
Forgiveness: Facing and Leaving Hell

Proverbs 14:10 says, "The heart knows its own bitterness" (RSV). Sometimes the things that life hands us are just too deep, too wretched, to put into words. You don't *have* to forgive. You might never be able to forgive; and if not, that's understandable.

However, so that you may clearly understand what forgiveness is and is not, let's explore a few thoughts. First let's look at what forgiveness is *not*, because many people have wrong assumptions about this subject. Many religious people blandly say, "Oh, just forgive your abuser, and then God will take away all your hurt." It's just not that easy.

If the Perpetrator Asks

Rarely, but occasionally, a perpetrator will say to a victim, "What will it take for you to forgive all this?" If this ever happens to you, it is your opportunity to give a few helpful hints such as:

- "Pay the bills for my therapy."
- "Come to therapy yourself, and then have some family sessions" (if your perpetrator is a family member).
- "Give a couple of years' volunteer time working in a service agency for abuse victims."
- "Give lots of your money to recovery programs."
- "Go through counseling and work on some of your own issues."

Suggestions such as these can be helpful to the victim, and they can at least open the door toward a perpetrator's getting help for himself. They may also lead toward the remote but possible thought of reconciliation.

FORGIVENESS IS NOT EVERYTHING

Let's imagine for a moment that you and I are standing facing one another. You are wearing heavy workmen's boots with steel toes. Suddenly, for no reason that I can understand, you kick me as hard as you possibly can in my left shin. Your kick is so violent that it tears my pants, creates a large rip in my skin, and exposes my bone. The wound instantly begins to bleed, and I hop around on one foot holding my shin. Using this example, let's explore a few things which forgiveness is *not*.

Forgiveness Is Not Forgetting

Some naive folks will give you a piece of useless advice: "Forgive and forget." The people who use it the most tend to have the least knowledge of what it means. One victim said, "Forgive? Maybe someday. Forget? Never!"

Within the first forty-eight hours of your kicking me it's not likely that I will forget it, whether or not I choose to forgive you. And ten years from now I'll probably still remember that one day you unprovokedly crashed your boot into my shin.

God didn't create us with a button we could press in order to forget. Some victims are able to temporarily "forget" by repression, but that's not healthy and not truly forgetting. It's just a mind game.

God gave us memory so that we could avoid putting our hand on a hot stove twice. Usually memory is a friend. It helps us recall where the grocery store is and when to brush our teeth. It helps us find our keys when we lose them. It helps us avoid bumping into the coffee table twice.

But when we're deeply wounded it also helps us to remember terrible things. We recall not only the activity but also the smells, sounds, touches, and so on. And forgiving doesn't make those memories go away.

Actually, only God can intentionally forget. The Bible says that when we confess our sins, He remembers them no more (Jer. 31:34). The rest of us don't have this aspect of memory.

Forgiveness Does Not Release Abusers of Responsibility

If you kick me in the shin, you are responsible for your act, whether or not I choose to forgive you. The person who sexually abused you is forever responsible for his actions. Whether or not he is prosecuted in this lifetime, he will one day stand before a very righteous, powerful, and all-knowing judge. God knows what your abuser did to you. God knows your abuser is responsible for what he did to you. You know it too. So does your abuser.

Even if you completely, totally, and freely forgive him, your abuser is still 100 percent responsible for what he did to you. He is not released from his responsibility or guilt.

Forgiveness Does Not Address the Cause of Pain

When you kicked me in the shin, you knew the reason. I didn't. I was an innocent bystander, and suddenly you mashed my shin with your boot! Even if I now choose to forgive you, I might not be blamed if I also step back a few paces from you and put a chair or a desk between us. Forgiveness doesn't fix anything that's broken between you and me. It only clears the air so that the issues between us, which first drove you to kick me, can be addressed in a less emotional atmosphere.

Forgiveness Is Not a One-Time Act

Tomorrow when I get out of bed and my shin still aches, I may have to reconfirm my decision to forgive you. My pain may feel even worse tomorrow than it does today, as my shin stiffens and a scab forms.

That's how pain is sometimes. I may have to forgive you several times until my pain and anger are gone. As recorded in Matthew 18:21, Peter asked Christ, "How often shall my brother sin against me, and I forgive him? As many as seven times?" (RSV). Peter was evidently miffed at someone. Trying to be generous, he nonetheless wanted some limitations on how far he had to extend himself.

Christ responded, "I do not say to you seven times, but seventy times seven" (v. 22, RSV). That's 490 times. I can only think of one reason why Christ would have said this. The deeper the pain, the more frequently one may have to forgive another—until the forgiver is convinced that forgiveness is complete.

A Serious Caution

Don't assume that the simple words "OK, I forgive you" are sufficient to accomplish forgiveness. Forgiveness is actually a very specific and measured exercise. The more tritely it is handled, the more useless it will be in your own healing.

When you forgive someone you must define specifically and accurately just what it is you are forgiving. You might decide not to tell that person that you are forgiving him; sometimes that's best. At times forgiveness is more for our healing than it is for another person's conscience. Unless your abuser comes to you, asks for forgiveness, and demonstrates repentance for his crime, you don't need to tell him that you forgive him. But you might want to forgive him for your own spiritual and emotional health.

In the Action Items at the end of this chapter there is a very specific exercise dealing with forgiveness. Treat it with the utmost respect. If you're going to do it lightly, don't do it at all. It will be a waste of your time. Now we will turn to a few benefits of forgiveness.

BENEFITS OF FORGIVENESS

Forgiveness is one of the most powerful clinical and spiritual tools available for healing. Its healing effect is almost beyond measure. However, before we begin to consider the benefits of forgiveness, consider the following serious caution.

Forgiveness Frees You from the Past

After abuse many victims spend time pondering what happened. Figuratively speaking, sticky spider webs seem to hold the victim to the memories and feelings of abuse. Forgiveness can be compared to a pair of scissors, cutting one free from those webs.

Forgiveness Frees You to Forgive Yourself

If you can forgive your abuser, you can forgive yourself. Factually you might not need forgiveness, because you were a victim. You were used. But emotionally you probably recognize a difficulty in forgiving yourself.

Many victims spend a lifetime castigating and punishing themselves. Forgiveness cleans the slates. It provides the opportunity for a new, fresh start.

Forgiveness Creates Dignity

There's almost no way to truly vindicate or even the score after abuse. It's such a nasty score to even! And even if there were a way, many victims simply would not have the heart to try to even the score. It's dehumanizing to do something that wretched, even in return for one's abuse. Revenge would put the victim on a par with the perpetrator himself.

However, victims often carry old feelings and memories into new relationships, and sometimes they find themselves lashing out at people who remind them of their abuser in some way. It's best to face the fact that you'll likely never get even, and it's not healthy for you to scheme and fantasize about doing so. Fantasizing about revenge or carrying deep animosity may give you an illusionary sense of personal power. But in the end what you carry with you will become part of your burden and therefore a waste of time and energy.

Forgiveness helps create dignity where once there was wretchedness. Forgiveness gives you the power to be stronger than your abuser. It breaks the hold he has on your emotions and memory. In forgiveness there is strength. In unforgiveness there is continued suffering.

Forgiveness Facilitates Personal Healing and Growth

As we have previously discussed, one of the major hurdles victims face is that of breaking out of denial and repression. Victims often struggle with the facts of their abuse. It's easier not to think about them because doing so is painful.

Therefore, part of healing is remembering. Only after remembering, being very specific about that which one chooses to forgive, and then forgiving, can one begin to feel the peace and joy of forgiveness. Forgiveness can create a deep sense of personal healing and open the door to personal growth.

ALLOW GOD TO FORGIVE

Victims often have a difficult time forgiving themselves. They're often good at self-punishment and self-hatred, but forgiving themselves often seems out of the question.

To process this idea of self-forgiveness, let's turn to a story from the Bible. John 8:3–11 begins with a few self-important public figures plotting to entrap Christ so they can discredit Him in front of His followers.

At that time the law said that persons caught and convicted of committing adultery were to be taken outside the city walls, and the townsfolk were to throw rocks at them until they were dead. This form of capital punishment was acceptable in those days.

To avoid frivolous accusations, the person making the charge was required to be first at throwing a stone. After that person did so, everyone else could join in. It was that culture's way of making sure that the accuser felt strongly enough about the accusation to be personally willing to participate in the death sentence of the guilty party.

The men in the story probably used one of their friends to seduce the woman. Then, probably at some prearranged signal in the midst of intercourse, the rest of them rushed into the house and "caught" her.

It would be useless at this point to focus anger upon the men who set up this situation. Obviously they were chauvinists who attempted to disguise their personal pathologies under a cloak of religious piety. (Some things never change.)

Let's focus on the woman—we'll call her Sharon—and Christ. Sharon was probably still very attractive, although we all tend to get "harder" looking when we are used by others. She was probably a hurt and lonely woman; most people who are readily available for sex are attempting to fill the loneliness they feel by sexuality.

She might well have been a victim. The men knew they could use her and she wouldn't rat on them—just like a victim. So they brought her before Christ, made her stand in front of the whole town, accused her, and humiliated her.

When Christ saw the situation He was so angry that He avoided speaking for a few moments. Instead, He stooped down and wrote on the ground. Then, standing up, He said, "Let him who is without sin among you be the first to throw a stone at her" (v. 7 PHILLIPS). Then He stooped down and wrote in the dust again. (Some commentators speculate that Christ was writing the names of other people who had used her—nice "upright" folk who should also be stoned to death: Bill . . . Tom . . . Charles . . . and so on.)

The Bible says that one by one, beginning with the oldest, they left. They all knew the whole thing stunk. They all knew that Sharon had been used again. Nobody in that crowd was innocent.

Now Sharon and Christ were alone. Sharon was probably expecting a lecture and further rejection and humiliation. But Christ asked, "Where is everyone? Didn't anyone accuse you?" Sharon said, "No one, sir." Christ then said the most freeing words you might ever read: "Neither do I condemn you; go, and do not sin again" (v. 11 PHILLIPS).

Christ didn't come to accuse us. He came to forgive us and to free us. God can handle our mistakes. Say that aloud: "God can handle my mistakes." Then say aloud: "God loves me. I am lovable. I am free to live again, just as Sharon was free to live again. I am clean. God loves me. He loves me."

The only hurdle between you and your freedom is you. Can you forgive yourself? Can you accept God's forgiveness and His love? If not, then ask yourself a very serious question. How much longer will you choose to punish yourself before enough is enough? Here's another, perhaps even deeper question. If you can't forgive yourself, how will you ever be able to love another person or to receive love from another person?

Let Go and Let God

This is one of those matters that's easy to say but hard to do. It's genuinely difficult for victims to trust that (a) God loves them as individuals and (b) letting go will make a difference for the better in their lives.

Victims usually find it hard to trust God. After all, didn't God allow the abuse to happen? If you wish to direct your anger at God, that's OK. God can handle your anger, and He is grieved and angered that you were abused.

However, when you turn your pain, memories, humiliation, and anger over to God, He can begin working His healing in your life. As long as you hold on, God can't fix what's broken—like a child asking a parent to fix her toy, but refusing to allow the parent to hold the broken toy.

What do you let go of? Well, try letting go of your feelings of failure. Then accept God's gift of acceptance. Try letting go of your self-hatred, and accept God's gift of respect. Let go of your rehashing and replaying all those memories, and accept God's gift of peace. You'll find that when you follow through with this difficult action, God gives you something good to take the place of what you've given up.

Try this exercise: Close your eyes and visualize putting all of the bad things into a balloon and floating them up to God. Then visualize God putting the good things into a cloud and gently raining them upon you. Do this exercise frequently. It is a form of praying.

QUESTIONS FOR REFLECTION

1. As you process the general subject of forgiveness, what is the most distasteful part of it? What aspect is the hardest, and why is it so hard?

2. In your heart of hearts, consider who needs forgiveness more—you or your abuser.

3. If you could do anything in the world to get even with your abuser, what would you do?

4. If you did as you wished (as expressed in question 3), what would it do to your own sense of self-respect and dignity? If you don't care about your self-respect and dignity, why not?

5. What is your definition of forgiveness?

=== ACTION ITEMS ===

1. Write three paragraphs about how choosing not to forgive keeps one more closely tied to the source of pain.

2. If you think you wish to forgive, but are not quite ready to do it, go to your calendar and circle a date in red. Make that your target date. Whether or not you ever tell your abuser that you forgive him, set this date for yourself to leave the past in the past.

3. For a month, begin each day with a short prayer asking God to help you forgive yourself.

4. Make up a multipage list of every grievance you have ever had against your abuser(s). Be very specific and thorough. Write down every tiny thing that your abuser(s) did to you, and record how each made you feel. Write the long-term effects the abuse has had upon your life. This is to be the most complete, vivid, and if necessary graphic list you have ever written.

After you have recorded all the pain, beside each item on this list that you can forgive now, use a red pen to write the words, "For *this* I choose to forgive you." Then sign your initials each time you write those words. In the months ahead, if you have any question about whether you have forgiven, you have a signed record. As you grow and heal, you have a written account of those grievances that you have not yet forgiven.

FOR SPIRITUAL GROWTH

1. Read Jeremiah 29:11. God is saying, "I know the plans I have for you" (RSV). Plans for goodness and wholeness. As you consider your healing, how does it make you feel to read that God has positive and healing plans for you? Are you willing to believe that God has such plans for you?

2. Read aloud the following prayer.

Oh God, this is a terribly difficult thing. For me to even consider forgiving my abuser makes me want to scream, "No! It's not fair!" I want to run away.

Part of me would rather lash out and get even. Part of me wishes I could hurt him as badly as he hurt me.

Lord, I know that if I were to truly give back even a portion of the pain that I experienced, doing so would reduce me to the level of my abuser. That is not something I will do to myself.

But forgive? How can I? Even if he were on his knees begging my forgiveness, part of me would rather spit in his face.

It's costing me "double," God. It cost me when he abused me, and now it's costing me to forgive. This isn't fair. I hate it.

And yet I am beginning to learn that this may be the only path out of some of my pain. I have to let go, and it doesn't make sense for me to let go of it in any way except by learning to give it to You.

I am finding that as I carry the acid of my anger and bitterness, that acid eats at my soul. It's costing me more and more, even as I pray this prayer.

How do I do this, God? How did Christ ask You to forgive those men who drove spikes into His wrists? It's beyond my ability to understand.

And how do I forgive a man who would sexually abuse me?

Oh, faith? Is that the answer? Faith? Am I to just trust that someday You will make recompense on my behalf?

But what if You don't? What if You forgive my abuser? I wonder if I could accept Your love for me if You forgave my abuser.

Lord, I didn't come here to fight. I've just got a lot of anger and pain inside me.

I'm going to stop fighting You. Teach me how to forgive. Help me experience the peace and joy that comes when I turn my pain over to You.

I give up, God. It's all Yours. I let go of it. I forgive. (I may have to do this a few times before I believe I'm even doing it. Please be patient with me, God.) I forgive. There. I've said it twice. I forgive.

I give it all to You. If You can do anything with this junk, anything to heal me, please have at it, because You know more than anyone how much I need healing.

Lord, I still remember what he did to me. I still ache and I still hate—well, I guess as much as anything, I hate myself. So I forgive my abuser. And I forgive me too.

Please love me, Lord. I need Your love so much. Let me lean on You. I'm giving up a lot here, and I need You to fill the emptiness left in my soul as I forgive.

As I allow the poison to leave my soul, please fill it with Your love. As I forgive, please put the salve of Your Holy Spirit upon my wounds. Amen.

Chapter 17
What About God?

A Victim's Prayer

Oh God, I am so torn. Things have happened to me that I wouldn't wish upon my worst enemy. I have been deeply wounded and grievously stained.

I find that trusting, really trusting another person, is pretty difficult for me. And if I can't trust people whom I can see, how can I trust You?

Why did You let these things happen to me, God? Why didn't You rescue me?

I am told that You love me. I'd like to believe that, but the word "love" is so polluted in my heart that it's hard for me to know what Your love for me may mean. In some ways I'm afraid of love, God.

Yet I need love. I need Your love. I know I need You to reach inside my trembling, wounded heart, way back behind my defenses, and put Your holy salve upon me.

It's so painful, God. It's so awful. I am so ashamed to even think about what happened. Can You love me? Are You really willing to love me?

I hope so, because without Your love I fear I may be completely lost and hopeless. Please love me. Please teach me what it's like to be loved by You. Please help me to love me.

Learning how to stand up for the person You created me to be will probably come later, God. I know I have not liked what You created when You made me. I have lived with too much pain to respect me. It's been a matter of survival for a long time, God.

I'm just asking for Your help right now. I'm reaching out to You, God. Amen.

One of the most difficult challenges for many victims is accepting the fact that God did not set them up for the abuse. The perpetrator always sets up the victim. Equally difficult for many is learning to separate God, the loving Father from the image of *father* or *male* as perpetrator.

While we're discussing males in general, perhaps you have questioned why a man has written this book for women who are sexual abuse victims. Both of these issues—God and a male writer—will be addressed in the pages that follow.

WHY DID VICTIMS COME TO ME?

I didn't set out to write this book. Actually, the circumstances just seemed to evolve. They began with a desperate phone call from a friend who had received an obscene phone call and was suddenly remembering things that had been repressed for years. She was deeply traumatized and needed to talk.

We talked and prayed for several hours. And that would have been the end of things, normally. But for some reason, it wasn't the end. We continued to talk together. Soon other victims joined us.

One key question I asked myself is, "Why did I accept the

invitation to work with women who were struggling with such profound issues? Why didn't I refer these women to a female therapist?" When one asks deep enough questions, sometimes one can get deep enough answers. Such was the case here.

One morning I had arrived early for an appointment, so I was sitting in my car reading the newspaper. One of the articles in the paper dealt with a husband and wife who had just been sent to jail for beating their children. Their children had been placed in foster care. When punishment seemed in order, this couple would make their children undress. Then they would beat the naked children with leather belts or razor straps.

At first I skimmed over the article. It was just another example of parents who were out of control and who were venting their clinical issues on their children. Then suddenly I stopped reading. My heart was pounding, and I was having very powerful memories of my own parents doing the same thing to me. I was remembering the humiliation of standing naked in front of Mother or Father, the fear of the belt or razor strap lashing my body, the pain of being whipped, the powerful feeling of being hated and rejected, and the sense that I was helpless and very, very bad.

This was standard fare in our household as I was growing up. In retrospect, this punishment was often given out for small infractions. After all, what horrible crimes could a six-year-old child commit to deserve being stripped and then whipped by a 225-pound athletic male?

Bingo! I too was a victim. As I read the newspaper article it dawned on me that I had been both physically and sexually abused as a child. (The last such beating occurred when I was thirteen years old, the year my father died.) Thus a puzzling situation began to make complete sense to me. I knew what humiliation felt like. I knew what it was to feel the rejection of those whom I needed to love me. I knew the shame and pain of these victims' lives. I'd been there too.

Furthermore, both of my parents had been extremely busy during my childhood years. They were gone much of the time, and their absence gave me the message that I was of little or no consequence to them. Their personal agendas were the order of the day. I grew up with some very real feelings of being left, abandoned. My father had been a compulsive workaholic, and my mother—the parent to whom a child naturally turns for emotional support and tenderness—was gone much of the time in support of my father's agenda. I was very much like the women whose fathers were abusing them and whose mothers were in some way absent.

Father and God

My childhood situation was especially confusing because the individual doing the whipping, rejecting, and abandoning was a minister. My father represented not only maleness and fatherhood, but also God. He was the one preaching on Sunday mornings. My mother was the one standing up front singing all those great old hymns with her fabulous operatic voice.

In the final analysis, as a child I believed that both my parents and God had become thoroughly disgusted with me. I came to believe that I was a very bad kid, one worthy of being stripped, whipped, humiliated, rejected, and then abandoned. I saw myself as being a loser, a weirdo, and an indelibly stained person, worthy of the hatred of others.

ONE VICTIM TO ANOTHER

That was the connection: one victim feeling the pain of another victim—one victim attempting to reach out and help another victim. The fact that I was male and the other group members were female was insignificant. We were all victims and spoke a very similar language.

Since that time I have had many other persons, women and men, come into my office and pour out their tales of horror and wretchedness. I saw the same struggles in the men that I had seen in many female victims—wretched embarrassment, humiliation, shame, anger, low self-esteem, feelings of abandonment, fear, deep struggles in establishing and maintaining intimate relationships, and feelings of being stained or dirty. I saw my own struggle.

SPIRITUAL WOUNDS

In the process of my own healing I discovered that the deepest wounds of all are usually the most spiritually significant. Indeed, I have concluded that all forms of human interactive pain are spiritual in nature.

For example, if you and I were close friends, yet I told other people some false, mean stories about you, you would be hurt. Worse, if I were to breach the trust you and I had in our relationship and tell other people true but embarrassing stories about you, you would feel betrayed.

If I were to overtly lie to you and occasionally attempt to manipulate money from you, I would place a heavy strain upon our friendship. If I were to kick and slap you and in general be abusive toward you, you would be wounded and begin to wonder if you could trust me at all. If I were then to be arrogant toward you, I would certainly stretch your ability to be my friend.

I have just listed several spiritually wounding items: bearing false witness, gossiping, lying, extorting, being abusive, and being arrogant. Did you know that God hates those kinds of choices? At one point in my life I didn't know that. I had grown up in a "Christian" home; I knew all about religion; and religion said that all of these things were wrong. But as a child I had been treated in such a manner *relationally* and *humanly* that when I was told that God didn't approve of people treating one another badly, these words meant nothing. These religious words were being spoken by religious adults, many of whom had used their religion to hurt me—all the while telling me that it was wrong to hurt others.

Spiritual Wounds and Moral Vacuum

If such "deeply moral" concepts mean nothing but words, then one might wonder if he has the ability to reason and act in a moral manner. When morality equals immorality, then a normal human response is often *a*morality, or *no* morality.

For example, when the word *love* becomes directly associated with the experience of abuse, then there is no positive meaning to the word *love*. Thus an abuse victim is left in a vacuum when attempting to discover what genuine love is all about. Some victims associate the word *love* with numbing themselves, either physically or emotionally.

Since what is learned is repeated, this vacuum becomes an adult life-style. Therefore, it is not too difficult to understand why many abuse victims struggle with promiscuity. Much promiscuity is a weak attempt by a person with an empty heart to feel at least some sort of "love"—or at least to attempt to break through some of the numbness. Among victims, sex is often the only way a person can feel any emotion other than anger or loneliness. Although not all sexual abuse victims are sexually active, many are trapped in a life-style called *promiscuous* that is merely a desperate attempt at finding love—a source of repeating numbing while attempting to connect.

When the word *commitment* becomes synonymous with the word *abandonment*, then there is no experience with genuine commitment. If there is no model of genuine commitment, then to consider being committed within a relationship becomes a fearful thing. "Am I able to commit my life to a spouse? Am I able to sustain such a commitment?" Many victims struggle with getting married, for making a lifetime commitment is an uncertain, sometimes frightening proposition. Many who do marry struggle with the fear that their spouse will eventually leave them. After all, why would anyone wish to be committed to a victim?

Spiritual Wounds and the Loss of Normalcy

A woman came to my office one day. She had been a victim of abuse at the hands of more than one family member. Her question was, "What is normal?" Speaking as one victim to another, one person without a true sense of what is normal to another person without a true sense of what is normal, I said, "I only have my own definitions of what is normal, and with my background I'm not sure I am a very good judge of what is normal. But I can tell you what I have learned about 'right' and 'good.' I can tell you what I have learned about what is health-producing. I can tell you what has helped heal me."

MEET GOD

Engaging in the healing process is often like walking around in a totally dark room filled with furniture, looking for a flashlight.

Such exploration results in bruised shins, tumbles over coffee tables, and bruised ribs. In my own bumping around, seeking wholeness and wishing to do what was right and good for myself and my family, I more or less stumbled upon something that has been of tremendous help to me, as respects God. You might suspect that I had some confusion about God, especially since my father had been a minister.

I had looked at God as pretty much an uninvolved Being, an uncaring and slightly mean person "up there" who, in occasionally looking down at me, seemed to enjoy making my life miserable. When He happened to catch me making my next mistake (of which there were many), I believed He enjoyed pouncing on me like a hungry cat on a field mouse, ripping me to pieces. As a victim, I always felt that I deserved that pouncing and ripping.

But I finally became hungry enough for God that I was willing to risk getting bashed by Him. I now recognize this as a reenactment of my quest for my own father, whom I wanted to love me. The message of my childhood had been, "If I get too close to Daddy he's going to hurt me. Still, I love and need him, so I'll have to risk the pain in order to get some of my needs met."

How does one go about getting to know God? All my life it had seemed that the doors of heaven had been slammed shut in my face. If it's true that we don't seek to truly change until the pain of not changing exceeds the pain of changing, then I had finally reached that point.

In a quiet, personal move of desperation I began reading through the Bible, again and again, cover to cover. At first I had no specific objective. I simply had no other place to turn. The Bible was the only tool I could think of to help me catch a glimpse of God.

I'm a slow learner, but one day a thought occurred to me. With my clinical orientation toward life, why not read through the Bible and attempt to discover what God wished for me in my personality and relationships? It was a shot in the dark that turned out to be a gold mine.

I began making a list of qualities that God desired in my personality and my relationships. Some words on that list included such beautiful thoughts as *trustworthiness, gentleness, peace, kindness, affec-*

tion, comfort, compassion, forgiveness, respect, sweetness of speech, and *mercy.*

After that particular read-through of the Bible, I had a list of about twenty-five items. I had enjoyed the exercise, but I was still hungry. In reading through the Bible again, I made a new list composed of characteristics that God hates in personality and relationships. Among the words on that list were *abusiveness, arrogance, brutality, deceit, ridiculing, spitefulness, violence, cruelty,* and *callousness.*

My lists are printed at the end of this chapter. Look them over now, and then return to this page.

Now let me introduce you to the character of God as I found Him through my own quest. The positive list is a composite, a word sketch, of the character of God. God is affectionate, blameless, comforting, compassionate, and so on.

In my muddled brain a new concept of God began to emerge. Maybe God wasn't the big bad celestial cat ready to pounce upon and tear up every little gray mouse in the field. Maybe, just maybe, God was nice.

Then one week I read through the book of Psalms again and almost tripped over one word that is applied to God's character more times in the book of Psalms than any other characteristic. If you had to pick one word to sum up everything that you think God is, what word would you choose?

Holiness? Perhaps. *Justice?* Maybe. *Power, omnipresence,* or *omnipotence?* Well, the word that I saw was *lovingkindness.* David, writer of most psalms, described God as being above all else *loving* and *kind.* And keep in mind that David said that about God in spite of David's having committed adultery and murder. David was no squeaky clean person who'd never sinned. *Lovingkindness.* How does that word strike you?

As I pondered the word a picture came to my mind: the woman of Luke 7:36–50, bent over the feet of Christ, crying uncontrollably in a room full of men, and wiping her tears from Christ's feet with her beautiful long hair. She obviously had a huge emotional load to bring to Christ. Perhaps she had done some things in her life about which she was ashamed. Perhaps she was a victim too. Whatever the reason, she was sobbing deeply, and it didn't matter that she was in a room full of powerful, rich, religious men. In that moment she was totally vulnerable, totally at the mercy of a man:

Christ. And in that moment Christ defended her against all the other men in the room. He was gentle, loving, and kind toward her. *Lovingkindness.*

The word sounded good to me. It suggested to me that perhaps all of the "God-talk" I had heard, particularly during my early years, had somehow missed the point. As an adult who has done a great deal of personal healing over the years, I have learned that any time one uses the word *God*, one must also in the same breath use the word *love*. And that word *love* has an identical twin named *kindness*. That is, God equals Love equals Kindness.

In creating my two lists I also discovered a definition of the word *love*. Many victims have asked me, "What does the word *love* mean?" Well, I finally figured it out. All of the words on the positive list make up a composite of the word *love* too.

I can't tell you what *normal* is. I'm not even sure that such a thing exists. But I can tell you that God is real, loving, and kind. He is able to do more to heal and restore you than anything else I know about. I can tell you that as you work at giving your life to God and changing yourself and your relationships to reflect the characteristics of the positive list, you will slowly begin to heal.

I can tell you one other thing about God. God really does hate for people to treat one another using characteristics from the negative list. When your perpetrator was abusing you, God was watching, was profoundly sad, and was deeply angry at the perpetrator. Consequently, in learning that God really hates such things as abusiveness and wickedness, I also learned that God is *just* and that there is such a thing as justice in the world. People might not always treat one another with justice, but there is a Being who will one day face off against the perpetrators of the world.

I learned that when the Scripture says of God, "'Vengeance is mine, I will repay'" (Heb. 10:30 RSV), He means business. And those who have sexually abused His children will one day face Him for their deeds. Put yourself in the perpetrator's shoes for just a moment. Can you imagine being a perpetrator and standing in front of God, who is justly accusing you of sexually molesting a child? Personally, I think I'd rather face a charging bull elephant than to be a perpetrator and face God.

Yet all is not clear, because some victims become abusers. Some children perpetrate upon others. And some who were abused found themselves returning for more abuse. The bottom line of God's character, as stated in the Bible, is that God is love.

Do you recall the story of the prodigal son? (Read Luke 15:11–32.) He went out into the world, spent his fortune, did all the wild living he could afford, and ended up feeding pigs to stay alive. Then he came to his senses and decided to go home, where the love is. The Bible says that while he was still far off, his father saw him and ran out to him, arms outstretched. God is love and will welcome you home when you come to Him.

VICTIMS AND GOD: A LITTLE HOMESPUN THEOLOGY

Many victims feel that God "set them up" for their abuse. Some believe that God put them into circumstances in which they could be abused, then let the abuse happen. Other victims believe that because they were bad to begin with, God allowed the abuse to happen to them.

When we are children and need help, we usually turn to our parents. If a bully is beating us up on the way home from kindergarten, we may run to Daddy for help. If a playmate is stealing our toys, we may ask Mommy for help. It's reasonable to turn to an authority when we need help. As we mature we learn that God is the ultimate authority.

Perhaps the ultimate irony is that God, in His absolute authority, has allowed human beings to do things His way or the wrong way. When we do things His way, life is generally happy and peaceful. When we do things the wrong way, life can become painful.

When one is a child, living in a situation in which a trusted adult is doing things the "wrong way" (abusing us), we may wish for God to step in and right the wrong immediately. God generally doesn't choose to take action in that way.

God chooses to allow many painful situations to occur. That's partially how He helps us learn to be responsible. He allows us to live with our choices and their consequences. That may seem inconsistent with a loving God when little children are allowed to be the objects of adults' sexual and aggressive pathology. Actually, when God created the world He knew that human beings would hurt each other. He knew we'd need a way to heal and get back on track again.

That's why God sent Christ, to offer pardon and reconciliation for people who did things the "wrong way." We *all* need a way to come back home after we've gone out and messed up. That's also why God provided the Holy Spirit, to help put salve upon the emotional and spiritual wounds that are inflicted upon us. The Holy Spirit is the only being who is tender and strong enough to both love me and heal me—and you. Through prayer I can reach out to God, and God will respond by sending the Holy Spirit to comfort me, heal me, help me forgive myself, and give me hope. That's much more than I can do for myself.

Would God Forgive a Perpetrator?

One might wonder whether her perpetrator could go to God and say, "I really messed things up. I'm a vile person. I sexually violated a child. I despise what I have done. I want to spend the rest of my life attempting to make amends for what I've done. I'd rather die than do anything like it again in my life. Please forgive me, or let me die." Would God forgive such a person?

The answer is yes. God is love, and God would forgive. However, the probability of such a person genuinely asking for God's forgiveness is remote. Sin tends to box us in and paint us into corners. The barrier of repression that helps some victims keep the memories of their abuse behind emotionally locked doors is the same barrier that keeps most perpetrators denying that they did anything wrong. As long as someone lives in that extreme state of denial, there's little chance that he will come to God, repent, beg for forgiveness, seek healing and reconciliation, and do anything possible to make amends.

If your perpetrator ever comes to you and begs forgiveness, you may be faced with the most challenging moment of your life. If you believe his plea to be genuine and sincere, the challenge will be to forgive him. It's an extension of the concept that while we were sinners (ourselves) and alienated from God, Christ died on the cross to give us access to God's *lovingkindness*. We are then challenged to offer reconciliation to those seeking it. That offer of reconciliation cost God a lot. It might cost us something too.

QUESTIONS FOR REFLECTION

1. In what ways is your image of God as Father tied up in conflictual and painful recollections involving males?

2. As you review the two lists at the end of this chapter, what thoughts and feelings emerge in regard to your image of God?

3. When you think of God as being *love*, what thoughts or feelings come to mind?

4. If you were to stand face to face with God right now, what favor would you ask of Him?

5. What would you do if your perpetrator(s) were to come to you and sincerely, honestly, with tears and deep remorse, beg your forgiveness?

6. What do you do when your perpetrator, your family, and any others who should believe you don't—when they want you to join in their denial of your abuse? To what source of truth, to what anchor do you turn?

FOR SPIRITUAL GROWTH

1. Various forms of child abuse have been around for thousands of years. Read Leviticus 18:21; 20:2–5; 1 Kings 11:7; 2 Kings 23:10; Jeremiah 32:35. How did these people abuse their children? In the verses immediately following each of these texts, what was God's opinion of those who abuse their children? What was God going to do about this abuse?

2. Read Psalm 18:35. What trait of God did the psalmist say made him great? How does that feel to you as a woman?

3. Read Psalm 25:9–10. Can you find four traits of God's character in these two verses? What are they?

4. Read Psalm 31:9–10. Do you think that David ever struggled with pieces of his own brokenness? As a woman, can you relate to such a cry to God?

5. Read Psalm 34:4–8. As a woman, what would it feel like to "take refuge in the Lord"?

6. Read Psalm 34:18. What does this verse promise you? How does that feel?

7. Psalm 63:6–7 suggests a peaceful activity for you to try when you can't sleep at night.

8. Are you worried about whether God will forgive you? Read Psalms 65:3; 86:5.

9. Read Psalm 89, and note how many times the psalmist talks about God's *lovingkindness*. What does that word mean to you?

Qualities God Loves in Personality and Relationships

Affection
Blamelessness
Comfort
Compassion
Contentment
Dignity
Discretion
Encouragement
Equity
Fairness
Faithfuless
Forgiveness
Gentleness
Good deeds (actions)
Goodness (character)
Grace
Graciousness
Honor
Hospitality
Humility
Innocence
Integrity
Justice (just anger)
Kindness
Knowledge of God
Love
Lovingkindness
Meekness
Mercy

Obedience to God
Patience
Peace
Peacemaking
Pleasantness
Praiseworthiness
Purity:
of Heart
of Mind
of Deeds
Respect
Respectfulness
Reverence
Self-control
Sensibility
Slowness to anger
Steadfastness
Sweetness of speech
Temperance
Tenderheartedness
Thankfulness
Trust
Trustworthiness
Truth
Truthfulness
Uprightness
Wisdom
Work

Qualities God Hates in Personality and Relationships

Abusiveness
Arrogance

Bitterness
Bitter words

Bloodshed
Boastfulness
Bribery
Brutality
Callousness
Conceit
Corruption
Covetousness
Craftiness (sneakiness)
Crookedness
Cruelty
Deceit
Destructiveness
Duplicity
(being two-faced)
Envy
Evil:
 deeds
 thoughts
 plans
Falsehood
False witness
Favoritism
Foolishness
Greed
Haughtiness
Hypocrisy
Immorality
Impurity
Injustice
Lying
Malice
Maliciousness
Maligning
Meanness

Murmuring (grumbling)
Oppressiveness
Partiality
*Pleasure loving
Pretense (making pretenses)
Pride
Pridefulness
Pugnaciousness (always
 looking for a fight)
Quarrelsomeness
Quick-temperedness
Rebellion
Religiousity (pretending
 to be a religious person)
Ridiculing
Scoffing
Selfishness
Self-righteousness
**Sensuality
Slander
Sloth
Spite
Spitefulness
Strife:
 strife-making
 strife-maintaining
Tale bearing
Treachery
Ungratefulness
Vengeance
Vengefulness
Violence
Wickedness
Worldly sophistication
Wrathfulness

*When *pleasure loving* becomes a life-style it usually also becomes degenerate. It becomes an end unto itself and is usually destructive.

**Sensuality is not in and of itself a sin. When a man and woman marry and make love they certainly enjoy being sensual. But when a perpetrator seeks sensuality with a child it's a different thing. When sensuality becomes a life-style it usually becomes destructive.

Chapter 18
Rebuilding a Life, Part I

I could never have known it would be this long or this difficult a journey. My wholeness turned out to be the major journey of my life. Yet I am discovering that I am worth all of it! *Hooray for me! I am worth all of it!*

Frequently the media will feature stories of people who have faced a major hurdle in their lives and have overcome the difficulty in heroic ways. Sometimes the stories are about athletes who, in spite of some severe handicap or major accident, become Olympians.

At other times the stories involve people who have faced imprisonment, torture, or cancer and have overcome it. We always cheer for these victors. However, there is a difference between seeking victory over matters that are "outside" oneself versus matters that are "inside."

Even though sexual abuse happens to the outside of one's

body, most of the damage is done deep inside the soul. In this chapter we'll focus upon specific items necessary to rebuild a life.

The rebuilding task requires that you use a tool that has been broken: yourself. You'll be asked to call upon a surgeon whose fingers have been broken, and you'll have to trust that surgeon's ability to cut and stitch. You are that surgeon. The task is challenging. Following are some skills you'll need to learn.

ASSESS YOURSELF SPIRITUALLY

Some people recognize a world of difference between spirituality and religiosity. You may wish to reject the word *religiosity* and all of its trappings in favor of the word *spirituality*. We are all created as spiritual beings, and God desires to have fellowship with us.

As we discussed in the last chapter, sometimes it's difficult to figure out what God is all about. For the moment let's leave our anger and philosophical questions at the door. Let's explore what God says, as His words and deeds are recorded in the Bible. In making a spiritual assessment it becomes immediately clear that God can handle our deepest pain. In fact, Jesus Christ's purpose is to take upon Himself our deepest hurts and to help us understand God's great love for us in spite of what may have happened.

Whatever else this may mean to you, it means at the very least that God loves you very much. Whatever you may or may not have done, you are forgiven and free. So much for the "easy," intellectual part. Now let's deal with the harder part: that voice inside you that says, "Yeah, but you're still stained."

If you've ever read the book of Job in the Old Testament, you'll remember that God calls for an assessment of creation and asks the spiritual beings of the universe to make a report. One of these beings is Satan. As God brags about the faithfulness of Job, Satan immediately begins to slander Job. Satan criticizes Job's character, claiming that the only reason Job loves God is that God has blessed Job so much.

The rest of the story involves Satan trying his hardest to destroy the relationship between God and Job. Satan begins and ends his task with slander—with Job, and also with you. Satan will use everything he can to accomplish three objectives:

1. *Separation from God.* He wants to separate us from God in any way possible.

2. *Separation from others.* He wants to separate us from each other, to force us to live in interpersonal isolation.

3. *Separation from ourselves.* He wants to separate us from our self-esteem and self-respect.

If you consider abuse and its effects, all three of Satan's objectives are accomplished.

Now read Romans 8:33–35: "Who would dare to accuse us, whom God has chosen? The judge himself has declared us free from sin. Who is in a position to condemn? Only Christ, and Christ died for us, Christ rose for us, Christ reigns in power for us, Christ prays for us! Who can separate us from the love of Christ?" (PHILLIPS).

Abuse victim though you may be, you are loved by God. God's assessment of you is evidenced by the cross of Christ, where the greatest possible statement of love was made. You are loved. God loves you. In spite of the hard things that have happened in your life, God loves you.

Consider Israel's great King David. He had a successful life in many ways, yet some hard things happened in his life. God loved David, but He did not stop King Saul from making several attempts to kill the young David. Nor did He prevent soldiers from killing David's son, Absalom.

Many victims feel as if they've been party to the ruination of their lives. Again, look at David. God was there to walk beside David, to offer friendship and to share in all of David's life, even though David really messed things up from time to time. God loved David, but He did not keep David from having an affair with Bathsheba or from murdering Bathsheba's husband. Can God love a person even after adultery and murder? Yes. God can do that. Can God love a person even after she is involved in a sexually abusive relationship? Yes, God can love that person too.

If you have children, would you hate them if they had been abused? Of course not! Nor does God hate you. God loves you even more than you love your own children, imperfect though they might be.

BREAK THE PATTERN OF NEGATIVE
SELF-TALK

Many victims fall into a cycle of self-abuse. It begins with negative self-talk: "You are so ugly." "I hate you." "You are really stupid." "You're nothing but a failure."

Your self-talk messages might not be quite as obvious as these, but most victims give themselves many such messages every day. They reinforce low self-esteem, but they're even more dangerous than that. We perform very much in accordance with how we think we will perform. Apply that concept to a victim's self-talk, and it becomes clear why many victims find themselves failing at tasks, relationships, and goals.

For your own benefit, decide to undertake a lifetime quest on your own behalf. The quest is that of *immediately* and *forever* ceasing to talk to yourself in negative terms, replacing that negative self-talk with *only positive talk*. Following are some examples of negative versus positive self-talk.

Example 1

Your boss complains that you didn't get a project done on time, and now he's under greater pressure because of it.

Negative self-talk: "Way to go, stupid. You never get things done on time. You're such a failure, and you're so disorganized! It's a wonder they keep you employed around here."

Positive self-talk: "OK, kiddo, things got a little hectic around here the past few days. But don't forget, the boss was giving you lots of extra things to do! No wonder you're behind on the project. Good thing you're smart and efficient! Go for it! You can do a good job on that project. I have confidence in you!"

Example 2

Your daughter, Carrie, comes home with a bad report card. She is crying and angry. She blames her teacher for not being fair with her.

Negative self-talk: "The only reason Carrie got a bad report card is that I'm such a lousy mother. If I had my own act together she'd be a better student. I'm a loser, and I'm making her into one too."

Positive self-talk: "I have been through so much—I know what she's experiencing. She's frustrated and sad and feels like a victim. What she needs right now is a nice long hug, a cookie, and a glass of milk. Then she and I will sit down and figure out how she can do better in school. I'm smart. I can help her."

Example 3

Your husband comes home in a dark mood and complains that you're fat, you don't cook well, and you are not loving anymore.

Negative self-talk: "Of course it's all true. I should lose about twenty pounds, but what's the use? And I should put more energy into good meals and being more attentive to his needs. I'm such a failure. I'm ugly, fat, stupid, and useless."

Positive self-talk: "Everyone has room for improvement. I do, and so does he. But he's in a bad mood, and I'm not going to let him pick a fight right now. I know I'm a good person."

By-Products of Negative Self-Talk

1. You see only the bad in yourself.

2. You reinforce all the negative things in yourself, so you tend to repeat the negative things.

3. You set yourself up for failure by mentally practicing failure.

4. You lure others into seeing and treating you as you see and treat yourself.

5. You tend to perceive others as viewing you in a negative manner also.

6. You destroy the credibility of others who wish to love you, accept you, and pay you compliments.

7. Little by little you become what you think about yourself.

8. You lose hope, and therein you lose control over the positive choices of your own destiny.

9. You become ever more the victim.

Try Positive Self-Talk

There are lots of ways to talk positively to yourself. Following are a few examples. "You did the best you could. Relax. If you want to try doing better next time, go for it. If not, you don't have to try." "You are lovable. Sure, you have room for improvement, but do you know anyone who doesn't?" "Your thoughts and feelings are as important and valid as anyone's." "You have a right to be respected." "You have a right to make decisions based upon your feelings and best judgments." "You are capable of handling anything you choose to handle." "You don't have to be perfect to be loved. You just have to be you."

The most powerful agent in how one views oneself is not *how one is seen by others. It is how one chooses to see oneself.* Most victims tie their self-esteem to the perceptions of others. This is a double trap, first in that the perceptions of others are seldom accurate, and second in that victims tend to assume negative perceptions. Victims usually think that others think or feel badly about them.

Negative self-talk is a trap. Nobody but you can break you out of that trap. You must stop whipping yourself. You must start being kind, forgiving, and nurturing to yourself. Only you can do this for you, and you must do it.

A Positive Focus

There is a verse in the Bible that can help you as you "reframe" your life—change the psychological and spiritual "frame" you put around yourself from a negative one to a positive one. Memorize the following verse (Phil. 4:8 NASB), and use it to evaluate your self-talk.

"Whatever is *true*, whatever is *honorable*, whatever is *right*, whatever is *pure*, whatever is *lovely*, whatever is of *good repute*, if there is any *excellence* and if *anything worthy of praise*, let your mind dwell on these things" (italics added).

Here's one last tip about self-talk. If you absolutely must say negative things about or to yourself, then use this verse's ratio of positive-to-negative reinforcement: eight to one. For every negative thing you wish to say to yourself, preface it with eight positives, as you see in the verse you just read.

STOP TRYING TO BE PERFECT, AND START BEING REAL

Ellen was an abuse victim: fondled and raped by her stepfather when she was eleven, and in later years fondled by her brothers.

She grew up with a strong drive to be perfect. She said, "I felt that the reason I was hurting inside was because I had been bad. I thought that if I could be perfect, the pain would go away."

She made straight *A*'s all the way through high school and college. She studied for a master's degree and made a 4.0 average in that school as well. But she couldn't stop the negative memories and feelings.

Through personal counseling and hard work with a group of incest survivors, she faced the burning issue of her abuse. One of the hardest tasks she encountered was ending her quest for perfection. She had wanted to be the perfect wife, but learned that her quest for perfection was alienating her from her husband. She had tried to be the perfect mother, and found that she was immensely controlling toward her children.

Victims often seek perfection in order to stop the pain or to avoid future pain. It doesn't work. Seeking perfection just sets you up for failure, because nobody's perfect. Instead, seek being real. It's much easier, and it's far better for you. Enjoy life as a journey rather than perfection as a destination.

CHOOSE TO HEAL

One of the most interesting stories in the Bible is found in John 5:1–9. Jesus was visiting a place where sick people waited for an angel to "stir the waters" of the pool. When that happened, the first person into the pool would be healed of his or her ailment.

Jesus stopped and spoke to a man who had lain beside the pool for thirty-eight years. Imagine waiting for thirty-eight years! Then Jesus asked him a question that seems absurd at first: "Do you want to be healed?" (v. 6 RSV).

Thirty-eight years. That's a long time for anyone to have unresolved pain, isn't it? How long have you had unresolved pain? "Do you really want to be healed?" is an apt question after all.

How about you? Do you really want to be healed? There is a legitimate time for grieving over what happened in the past. There is a time for reflecting, for being angry about a mother who didn't protect or nurture. There is a time for sadness over lost innocence.

There is a time for fear of sexual arousal because of the memories it conjures up in one's mind. There is a time for depression because of a lost childhood.

But when does it stop? When is enough self-hatred enough? When is enough blaming enough? When does life begin again? There is a time to heal. You didn't choose to be a victim, but you have to *choose* to heal. It doesn't just happen.

You have to make a commitment to yourself: next week at this time, you're going to have taken some steps toward your own wholeness and happiness. You have to declare that today, tomorrow, and every day for the rest of your life, you will accept and love yourself.

Perhaps you're not finished grieving yet. That's OK. Perhaps you're not finished being angry yet. OK, fine. But *when* will you choose to begin believing that things can be different for you?

Jesus was right. The man needed to answer the question. He started out by making some excuses, by saying that his inability to heal was the fault of those around him. He complained that when the angel came to stir the water, nobody put him into the pool.

This is victim-talk. Victims are helpless. Are you helpless? Or are you capable of starting and maintaining the journey of your own healing? When are you going to start nurturing yourself? When are you going to start trying to love that little girl who was abused— that little girl who still hates herself because of what she's been through? Christ was right. One has to choose to heal. You too have to choose. (Read John 5:8–9 for the happy ending to the sick man's story.)

QUESTIONS FOR REFLECTION

1. If someone were to listen to the way you talk to yourself, what would he hear? How's your self-talk? List three common themes you use in talking to yourself.

2. Reflect upon forgiveness. Specifically, reflect upon forgiving three persons: your mother, for not rescuing you; your abuser(s), for what he (they) did to you; and yourself. Who will be the hardest

to forgive? Why? What thoughts might you need to release to God in order to forgive? Write these items down on paper.

3. Reflect upon how you invite others to despise you. How do you do this? How does self-hatred become a self-perpetuating downward spiral? Reflect upon why you choose to live within this spiral.

4. If healing is really a choice, why do some people choose not to heal? What advantages are there in not healing? Can you name three advantages in not healing?

5. What's the most difficult part of accepting the challenge of healing? Write it down. Reflect upon why this is difficult, painful, or challenging to you.

═══ ACTION ITEMS ═══

1. Write a love letter from God to yourself. Pretend that you are God, writing to a beloved child. Make the letter at least three pages long.

2. Every time you catch yourself trying to be perfect this week, stop and write one short paragraph about what you are doing and why.

3. After you have written five such paragraphs, read them and try to determine if you have been using some pattern of avoiding pain, fear, or sadness by your quest for perfection.

FOR SPIRITUAL GROWTH

1. Read Luke 7:36–50. Then reflect upon this text in the following way:

   a. Put yourself into the picture as the woman.
   b. Assume that she was a sexual abuse victim; she well may have been.
   c. Assume that her tears came from sadness, guilt, and a great need for cleansing.
   d. Consider the assumptions of the self-righteous men in the scene. Name some of these assumptions as you read through the story. Are these types of assumptions made by people in our culture today? If so, how do they affect you as a victim?

e. Who is defended in this story?

f. What's the high point of the story, as found in verse 47?

g. What's the last thing that Christ says to the woman? How does that message apply to you?

Chapter 19
Rebuilding a Life, Part II

In this chapter you'll find more healing skills.

FACE THE WORST POSSIBLE SCENARIO

Most victims worry a lot. Many worry that they might have been seductive. Others worry that they cannot remember everything that happened to them, and they fear the worst. For many victims, part of healing may require painting a "worst-case scenario" picture for themselves, facing it squarely, and then choosing to move on.

What would be the worst thing you could imagine about your abuse? Perhaps it might be that you actually were seductive or that you in some way asked for what happened. It might be that you had sexual feelings during your abuse and therefore feel ashamed. Or your worst fear might have to do with specific sexual acts.

Whatever your greatest fear may be, go ahead and imagine it. Create a mental scene in which your worst fear actually comes true. Devise your own worst-case scenario. You have to stop the madness sometime, and now is the time. As you work on your healing right now, that which actually happened to you in your abuse is less important and significant than *your adult ability to heal.* What matters at this moment is that you develop some skills to intentionally move yourself forward in life.

It might be helpful for you to take paper and pencil and write your worst-case scenario on paper. As you write, make it as explicit, as frequent, and as intentional (on your part) as you need to in order to convince yourself that "this is as bad as it ever was or could have been."

After you've written it all down, get a big red felt-tipped pen. Write in bold letters upon your worst-case scenario, "Even if all this is true, I now release it to God, and I now forgive myself."

ESTABLISH CLEAR BOUNDARIES IN ALL RELATIONSHIPS

Healthy personal boundaries are very important. To understand the word *boundaries,* used in this sense, imagine that you live on an island in the ocean. The boundaries of your existence are where the sand reaches the water. You own the island. Everything you need is on the island. You can invite visitors, and you can demand that people leave. You are the queen of the island, and your word is law.

One day an evil man comes to your island uninvited. He has just breached your *physical* boundaries.

While on the island, he breaks down several of your favorite trees, rips your grass hut, sets fire to your garden, and rapes you. Now the man has breached your *personal* boundaries.

Any time a person enters your life in a manner that is invasive, in a manner that makes you feel uncomfortable, and does things that frighten or hurt you, that person is breaching your boundaries. That which is supposed to be safe (your personal space, values, thoughts, and body) becomes unsafe. You are invaded and either emotionally or physically wounded.

That's what happens when a child is sexually abused. Her personal boundaries are breached. This breaching is so traumatic that it often takes decades for her to feel safe and whole again.

As you heal you must learn that it is not only OK but imperative for you to build and maintain firm boundaries in all relationships, even in intimate relationships. You must be able to rely on them when you need them. You must be confident that you can exert your own power to keep people out whenever you feel threatened, disgusted, manipulated, hurt, or sad. You must be able to let people in, or not, *at your discretion, when you feel like it, for your own reasons.*

In your new life as a *survivor,* you'll assign people different boundaries. It's your choice. Nobody can force you anymore. You're an adult woman now.

If you're uncomfortable with a certain person, you may now tell that person you are uncomfortable. You may physically move away. You may put a barrier between the two of you. If someone is attempting to manipulate or force you to do something against your will, you now have the right and the power to say, "No! Stop! You may not do this to me!"

If you are feeling angry or frightened, you now have the right and the power to take action to address your feelings. You now have the power to establish and maintain clear boundaries, and you must do so if you wish to heal.

AVOID COMMON VICTIM PITFALLS

Pitfall 1: Waiting for someone else to help you heal. It's not possible for someone else to heal you. Those who say they can heal you are setting you up for a codependent relationship. Others can only love you (if you'll allow them to love you, if you'll trust their love for you) and (perhaps) show you the path of healing.

Pitfall 2: Quitting on yourself. Many victims just give up. "It's too hard. I can't keep trying. I'm not worth the struggle." If you quit on yourself, then you'll continue to live the rest of your life as a victim. Is this what you want?

Pitfall 3: Denying your perceptions, thoughts, and feelings. Most victims have a hard time believing that what they see is accurate, what they think is valid, and what they feel is all right. During their abuse victims learned not to trust their judgment. They learned to see life through the eyes of denial, through the perspective of the abuser. Healing requires that you learn to trust and validate your own internal compass.

Is it good to hide your real feelings, mistrust your real thoughts, and question your perceptions to be accepted by others? Or is it better to start learning to be honest with yourself and with others?

As you ponder this thought you may find you fear that if you're honest, you'll lose the friendship of the few people you now have as a support system. Actually, the reverse is true. You will make more friends if you allow the "real you" to come out of your shell.

Pitfall 4: Running away through activity. Filling your life with "busyness" can be a very effective way of avoiding being alone with yourself and your feelings. If you're too busy to do anything but eat, work, and sleep, then you don't have to face some of the deep feelings inside such as anxiety, depression, anger, fear, and sadness.

Of course, the more you run away, the more you have to run away. It's like trying to run from your shadow; the faster you run, the faster it comes after you. Healing is facilitated when you allow yourself to slow down, think, feel, remember, and process.

Pitfall 5: Avoiding or misusing sex. Some victims attempt to use sex to enhance their shattered sense of self-esteem. Some use it as a hoped-for path to intimacy. Others stay as far away as possible. As you heal, if you have been promiscuous you will need to learn that neither sexuality nor emotional intensity is the same as love or intimacy. It is possible to have caring relationships without sex. Conversely, if your abuse has driven you to be pretty much asexual, you may need to accept that you are a woman, with sexual feelings and drives.

It's normal for sex to produce anxiety in abuse victims. It's hard to know what is right. To understand what is right and what works best in the long run, the best solution is the prescription found in the Bible: keep sex for the marital union only. Sex outside marriage is counterproductive to long-term intimacy. On the other hand, healthy marital sex is one of the strongest bonding agents between a man and a woman.

Pitfall 6: Hiding out until the pain stops. Some victims go into an emotional/relational cocoon and never come out again. It's possible to do this even within marriage, although doing so does not make for good, healthy marriages. This approach to healing is nonproductive.

To heal, one must decide to reengage in healthy relationships. Human beings are built for relationships. Prisoners who are incorrigible are often sent to solitary confinement. This punishment is so powerful that it will usually break even the most unruly prisoner.

There is some question as to how long a person can "hide out" and still retain sanity. Too much isolation often makes us a little weird. If you are using this as a coping mechanism, ask yourself two questions: (1) How long will you allow your perpetrator to control and ruin your life; and (2) how happy are you in your hiding?

Pitfall 7: Turning to drugs or alcohol. It is possible to use alcohol or drugs to temporarily numb pain, but this is not a healthy way to live. This approach creates more problems than it solves. If you're using drugs or alcohol to cope with your abuse, you need to seek help. Your life is worth saving. Your abuser is not worth the cost of your future.

LEARN TO LIVE BY YOUR OWN "BILL OF RIGHTS"

One survivor said that the only difference between a bucket of manure and herself was the bucket. For many victims, self-esteem is often a word applied to other people. Victims often don't believe they have much worth. A "Personal Bill of Rights for Survivors" follows; it was written by a victim-turned-survivor.

Personal Bill of Rights for Survivors

1. I have a right to numerous choices in my life beyond mere survival. I am not limited to the choices of others or to one choice.

2. I have a right to discover my Child within—the child brought from the past, into the light of today's sunshine.

3. I have a right to grieve over what I didn't get that I needed, or what I got that I didn't need or want.

4. I have a right to follow my own values and standards.

5. I have a right to recognize and accept my own value system as appropriate for me.

6. I have a right to say no to anything when I feel I am not interested, not ready, it is unsafe, or it violates my values.

7. I have a right to dignity and respect.

8. I have a right to make decisions.

9. I have a right to determine and honor my priorities, wishes, needs, and dreams.

10. I have the right to have my needs respected by others.

11. I have the right to terminate conversations with people who make me feel put down or humiliated.

12. I have the right to make mistakes, and not to have to be perfect.

13. I have the right to not be responsible for others' behavior, actions, feelings, or problems.

14. I have a right to expect honesty from others.

15. I have a right to be angry at someone I love.

16. I have a right to all of my feelings.

17. I have a right to be uniquely me, without feeling that I'm not good enough.

18. I have a right to feel scared and to say, "I'm afraid."

19. I have a right to experience and then let go of fear, guilt, and shame.

20. I have a right to make decisions based upon my feelings, my judgments, or any reason that I choose.

21. I have a right to be happy.

22. I have a right to change my mind at any time.

23. I have a right to stability, roots, and healthy relationships of my choice.

24. I have the right to my own personal space and time needs.

25. I have the right to cry, and not to have to smile as I cry.

26. I have a right to be relaxed, playful, and frivolous.

27. I have the right to improve my communication skills so that I may be understood.

28. I have the right to change and grow.

29. I have the right to be flexible and to be comfortable with my flexibility.

30. I have the right to live in a nonabusive environment.

31. I have the right to be healthier than those around me.

32. I have a right to make friends and be comfortable around people.

33. I have a right to take care of myself, as I wish.

34. I have the right to grieve over actual or threatened losses.

35. I have the right to trust others who earn my trust.

36. I have the right to forgive others and to forgive myself.

37. I have the right to give and receive unconditional love.

WORK AT TAKING CARE OF YOURSELF

Victims often attempt to make up for negative feelings about themselves by taking extra good care of others. The covert bargain might read like this: "If I, the victim, take good care of others, then those others will be obligated to like me, maybe a little bit (please?), and then maybe they won't reject or leave me (I hope), and then maybe I'll feel a little better about myself (but I doubt it)."

Dr. Bobbie Reed wrote the book *Pleasing You Is Destroying Me: How to stop being controlled by your people-pleasing habits.* The chapter titles are excellent mottoes or themes for victims' lives. They follow: "Take stock—become more open. Examine your life-style. Review your relationships. Identify your challenges. Speak up—become more honest. Express your opinions. Confront productively. Ask for what you want. Refuse unreasonable requests. Reach out—become more caring. Initiate contact. Give and receive compliments. Show love and affection. Love life—become whole. Set and achieve life-changing goals. Live free." One victim observed, "If I could learn to do all of those things, I wouldn't be a victim any longer, would I?"

CHANGE YOUR MENTAL POSTURE

In counseling with victims I ask them to create a mental picture of a "victim": helpless, exposed, vulnerable, humiliated. I then challenge them to use anger to release themselves. Then they are to dress and arm themselves with their own strength to protect and defend themselves against further victimization.

Catherine was mentally practicing this one day while her car was being repaired. The service station mechanic was calling her "Little Lady," "Toots," and other chauvinistic names. She described the incident as follows:

I was sick and tired of being treated as if I were a toy doll or a helpless little girl. I was a mature woman. I had a responsible job with authority over several people. How could this man dare to speak to me like this? In the past, because of my being a victim, I would have just internalized my feelings and then left the service station angry and hurt.

I said to him, "Who's the owner of this station?" He told me, and then he asked why I wanted to know. I told him I was going to write letters to the owner and to the district manager of the service station chain, complaining of the way I was being treated by a mechanic who thought he was a big shot.

It felt good to say that, so I took the next step and said, my voice rising to a high pitch, "And if you don't stop talking to me like I'm some stupid child I'm going to take that hammer over there to your thick head!"

I could never have done the latter. I fully intended to do the former. He meekly said, "Ma'am, I apologize for being rude."

How's your mental posture? Do you see yourself as a poor, helpless victim or as having choices and rights?

TRUST YOUR OWN INTERNAL COMPASS

Betsy grew up with parents who were both extremely invasive. They would invade her space no matter where she was. If she was in the bathroom, they would ask what she was doing. If she was in the shower, they would enter and ask if she was using the correct soap or shampoo. There was no privacy for her. Either parent would walk into her bedroom without knocking, and several times she was deeply embarrassed at being caught completely undressed.

Although she was never sexually touched by either parent, she was sexually humiliated until she left home at age twenty-two.

She's now thirty-five, has a Ph.D., and is a very attractive woman. But she's still wondering if she sees life the way it really is. She's still doing "compass checks," asking questions about what's normal. "Is it right for me to be angry when someone treats me with arrogance?" "Was it right for them to insist on being in the bathroom while I was showering and drying?" "If I don't like a man, do I have to go on a date with him?"

Ginger's mother lived in profound sexual denial. Ginger now believes that her mother and father may never have had intercourse; she may have been adopted. Her father handled his sexual needs by talking to Ginger about every possible aspect of sexuality. The conversations were embarrassing for her. She too is a sexual abuse victim although she was never physically violated. She too is still checking her compass to figure out what is normal, healthy, and appropriate.

If this is true of two women who were never physically sexually violated, it is also certainly true of victims who were. Victims lose trust in their own internal compasses. Sexual abuse is so demeaning that it usually shakes a victim's deepest sense of right and wrong. As if an internal earthquake had occurred, there is deep and profound damage done to one's navigational system.

As a result, many victims go through life asking such questions as, "Can I trust myself? Are my feelings valid? Is life actually as I see it? Do I have the ability to think? Is what happened to me 'right'? Is my internal compass right when it tells me that my abuser is wrong?"

Healing requires learning to trust your compass. Believe in your perspective. Feel what you feel, and believe that whatever you feel is both correct and accurate for you. Trust your ability to think and make decisions. Build your life around your own internal compass and what it tells you rather than around what others say you should be thinking, feeling, or doing. Your life should be lived by your compass.

QUESTIONS FOR REFLECTION

1. Can you remember one experience in which you had a strong emotion but denied it by making a joke about it, suppressing

it, or in some other way internalizing it? What was the emotion, and how did you discount or deny it?

2. Do you tend to discount the validity of your own feelings very often? Is it possibly a life pattern? If so, write a page or two about how it feels to consistently discount your own feelings.

3. Victims frequently find it very difficult to trust others. Is this a theme in your life? If so, write two pages about why it is difficult for you to trust. Then write one page about how you might begin to learn to trust others.

4. This chapter dealt with several measures of taking care of yourself. Do you take care of yourself? If not, why not? Is it because you are a victim? Write two pages about why you don't take care of yourself, your needs, or your feelings.

5. Reflect upon your own worst-case scenario. What is your greatest fear about your abuse? Write one page about this.

6. What would it take for you to rebuild the walls of your own personal boundaries so you could feel safe again? Is there anyone in your present life who bashes through your walls? If so, how does this person do it? Must you let this person do it?

═══ ACTION ITEMS ═══

1. Choose five statements from the "Personal Bill of Rights for Survivors" that are most significant to you. Copy them and hang the page on your refrigerator or on your desk at work. Look at them several times a day. Make them "yours" by learning to live them out in your life.

2. Write two pages about how you have learned to take care of others, but don't take care of yourself. Afterward share these pages with a close female friend. Ask her to help you become better at taking care of your own needs and less tied to meeting the needs of others.

FOR SPIRITUAL GROWTH

1. Read Psalm 139, paying special attention to verses 13–16. Reflect upon the wonder of yourself as seen through God's eyes.

2. Read Psalm 22:9 and reflect upon when a trust relationship ended for you. How can you rebuild trust in your own life and relationships?

3. Read Psalm 8:3–6. Reflect upon the authority and power that God has given to humanity. How do you fit into that picture, and how is your personal, God-given power related to your healing?

Chapter 20
Telling the Tale / Having a Setback

Once I started talking about my abuse it was as if a floodgate had been opened. It flowed for a long time. I wondered if my friends were getting tired of hearing about it. But it felt so good. The secret was finally coming out.

I found I was taking one step backward for every two I took forward. But I was finally moving forward!

In this chapter we'll explore various aspects of telling your story. We'll also explore having setbacks in the healing process.

Telling your story does one thing that your perpetrator attempted to disallow: it gets the ugly story out of the closets into the light of day where it can be seen—and healed.

Generally it is not in your best interests to keep your story hidden away but to start telling a few close friends about what happened to you. And eventually, it is probably in your best interest to personally confront your perpetrator.

SHARING YOUR STORY

Secrecy is essential for perpetrators. They fear the light of truth. They usually do a good job of putting their victims in a position of secrecy and isolation from help. Victims often believe that secrecy is in their best interest as well. "What if someone found out that I was sexually abused? They'd reject me!" "What if my humiliation became public knowledge? I'd just want to die!" Let's process a few thoughts in this regard.

Flashing Versus Sharing

Some people share their darkest secrets as if they were displaying badges of courage. I call this _flashing_, and it happens when a stranger sitting at a bus stop unloads her tragic story in what feels like an exploitive manner. "Did you know that when I was two years old I was raped by a motorcycle gang and sold into white slavery?" Flashing one's story is not genuine intimacy; nor is it what this chapter is about.

It is good to share one's story with close friends, in appropriate circumstances, quietly and with feeling, for the purpose of allowing a friend to know one better—perhaps leaving out some of the explicit details but being relatively open and complete. Telling your story is necessary in the process of reestablishing trust and in discovering that one can share such information and still be loved.

There is a dark question in most victims' minds: "If I truly open up and share my whole story, will anyone love me?" The answer is yes, absolutely. They will still love you. Every victim with whom I have worked has feared this loss of love, and every one without exception has found that, if anything, her friends loved her even more after she shared her story.

Some victims fear that telling their story will evoke feelings of pity and charity in others, and they don't want relationships built upon pity. If this is your concern, you need not worry. People will not respond to you with pity if you don't ask for it. You can share your story with strength and self-respect, even with tears, and people will love and respect you without feeling a need to "fix" you with their pity.

With Which Friends, in Which Circumstances?

One victim asked, "So do I walk into a group of friends at a dinner party and say, 'Hi, everybody! Guess what happened to me when I was twelve?'" You'll know when the time and circumstances create a good opportunity. There will be times when you are alone with friends and are able to say, "I'd like to tell you something about myself that I've kept tucked away for most of my life. I'm not telling you this so that you'll feel sorry for me, but so I can begin to get it out of the basement of my life and into the light of day."

Occasionally a friend may shed a tear as you tell your story. That's called compassion, and it's healthy. Your friend may say things like, "I never knew! I'm so sorry for you! What a terrible thing!" If you hear those kinds of words, then simply say, "I'm doing OK now, but it's been a rough journey." And then ask, "Now that you know this about me, do you still care for me as a friend?"

From virtually every person you'll hear something like, "Of course I still care for you! Why would I not care for you? If anything, I feel closer to you now because you have trusted me with this part of your life."

With Women and Men?

It's wisest to start sharing with close same-sex friends. As time passes you might find a man or two with whom you may feel comfortable sharing your story. If you are dating someone, I'd advise you not to share your story until you are quite sure your date won't respond to your story in a voyeuristic manner or use your abuse as his excuse to become sexually active with you.

One victim told of dating a man for a few weeks and sharing her story. They were out for dinner, and she said a reduction of the conversation went something like: "I was sexually abused when I was a child," and her date responded with, "Gee, too bad. Let's go to bed and I'll show you how to do it right." She called a cab.

With Family Members?

Again, the answer is generally yes. One victim found that as she shared her story with her sister, her sister began crying and said that the same thing had happened to her, by the same perpetrator—their stepfather. Another victim shared her story with her siblings, and one brother told her that he'd seen the perpetrator abusing another sibling. The two of them were able to begin working together for the healing of a third sibling.

But it doesn't always work that way. A family came to my office for counseling. The wife was a victim, and now their daughter had become a victim. The wife's father, grandfather of the child, was the abuser in both cases. When this couple went to the siblings with information about Grandfather, they were all but run out of town on a rail.

The interesting thing about this situation was that the grandfather was widely suspected in his small town to be an abuser, yet he was a well-known, highly respected church board member. The family system didn't want to deal with the truth, so it galvanized around the abuser and rejected the victims. That can happen. But let's put the emphasis where it belongs: upon truth and integrity.

CONFRONTING THE PERPETRATOR

You have no responsibility to protect your perpetrator from the knowledge that you know and remember what he did to you or from the knowledge of how his actions have affected your life. Your role in life is not to protect your abuser.

Most victims fantasize about confronting their abuser, watching him grovel, and then leaving him behind, his abusive actions exposed to the world for all to see. Should a victim tell her abuser that she clearly remembers what he did to her and what his abuse has done to affect her life? Absolutely yes, if she wishes to do so. Not all victims wish to confront their perpetrator, but most do; and it's very appropriate.

Should I "Let Sleeping Dogs Lie"?

Most victims ask this question of themselves, especially if their abuser was a family member. The abuser carries the adult responsibility of admitting, apologizing, and begging forgiveness for what he did. If he asks forgiveness, then you may decide whether to forgive him and let the issue go with him to his grave, forgive him but tell the world what he did to you anyway, or not forgive him. If he has abused other victims and is serious about repenting, let him voluntarily go to them and beg forgiveness.

However, few abusers ask forgiveness. Most choose to live in complete denial of their actions. Open communication about the abuser may help prevent him from causing greater harm in the lives of other victims.

Who Should Initiate Conversation with the Abuser?

I have yet to see a perpetrator who, on his own initiative and with no threat hanging over his head, comes to the victim and asks forgiveness. Every confrontation between victim and perpetrator that I have seen has been initiated by the victim.

Yet I have seen a few perpetrators break down in tears and tell their victims that they have despised themselves for what they did and have begged forgiveness. One victim said that when this happened she had a hard time managing her feelings, but she left feeling somewhat more healed than she did when she arrived.

How to Confront

There is no one right way to confront an abuser. Each victim must decide what is appropriate for her. Kitty grew up with an uncle and aunt, both of whom were extremely abusive toward her. The uncle was sexually abusive, and the aunt was verbally and emotionally abusive. At first Kitty didn't want to even be in their presence, so she wrote a long letter to her uncle. She also wrote letters to her sisters and followed up with telephone calls. She discovered that her uncle had abused at least one other sister.

Sandy decided to take a friend along with her to her abuser's home, knock on the door, and speak openly and directly to him and his wife. Jill called a family meeting and exposed her abuser in front of everyone. Ali wrote a letter, photocopied it, and sent copies to everyone in her family. Anne drove over to her brother's home (he was her abuser) and confronted him alone.

Once the Perpetrator Has Been Confronted

It's anybody's guess as to what will happen. Most perpetrators attempt to deny their actions. Kitty's uncle told everyone that Kitty had been on drugs, attempting to discredit her so that nobody would believe her story. Sandy's abuser admitted his wrong and asked forgiveness. At first Jill's family attempted to deny the truth. But finally enough evidence was accumulated from enough sources that they all joined together and confronted the abuser. Ali's family totally rejected her, choosing to live in their denial. Anne's brother wept openly and begged her forgiveness.

Why Bother?

There are two reasons why confrontation can be important. First, the perpetrator now knows that his quest for silence has been broken. If nothing else, this may make him act more responsibly toward other potential victims. If his actions become public knowledge, much pain in the lives of others could be prevented.

Second, confrontation allows the victim to say aloud, perhaps in public, all that has happened to her. It gets the truth into the open. And this is a justifiable motivation for confrontation and exposure of a perpetrator.

Sexual abuse is a crime. Although it may have happened years ago, exposing the crime to the healing light of public scrutiny is appropriate. There is something healing in a victim standing before her perpetrator and saying aloud, "You did this to me. You are responsible."

Don't Go It Alone

If you decide to confront your perpetrator, don't go through the whole process alone. You may or may not choose to confront him alone, one on one, but be sure to have a mature woman friend waiting for you when you come home. Choose someone you can cry with, someone you know well and trust deeply.

If you are afraid of confronting your abuser alone, then bring a woman friend along with you. You might even tell her every detail of your abuse so that if you come unglued in the middle of the confrontation, she can help you get back on track again.

Whether you take a friend or not, write a few notes on paper. Take them with you so you can remember all you wish to deal with; stressful situations affect short-term memory. You might forget or overlook something important, so jot down what you want to cover in the conversation.

Finally, plan how you're going to take care of yourself after the confrontation. You might want to go out for a nice dinner, have a good workout, or go home and cry alone for a while. But before you confront your abuser, have some sort of notion as to how you will take care of yourself for a day or two after the event. Have a "be nice to me" plan that you don't have to think about too much—something you have already planned and can do "on autopilot."

TAKING A STEP BACKWARD

Each victim engaged in the healing process has had temporary setbacks, points of taking one step forward and three steps backward. Most victims have several setbacks. This is normal. Expect it, but don't allow it to discourage you. By all means don't let it stop you from working on your healing. Following are some comments from other victims regarding setbacks.

I thought I was doing so well, and then I went back home to visit my parents. I saw him again, and now I'm back on the emotional roller coaster.

I was in a shopping center and a man brushed against me. I knew he was doing more than just walking past me. I first got scared, then mad; but now I can't stop thinking about what happened to me when I was a child. Why can't I get over this? It seems like I'm doing worse now than I was last month!

My husband and I were making love recently, when all of a sudden, seemingly out of the blue, I began to recall what happened to me when I was little! I hate this! Why does this happen? I thought I was doing so well, and now this!

Every time this happens to me—every time I take a step backward, I feel so guilty about it! What's wrong with me?

If you don't have setbacks in your recovery process, you might be the only woman in the history of sexual abuse recovery who has not. Relax. It's very normal. Avoid thinking like a victim: don't go on a guilt trip about it. Don't start punishing yourself again. Don't assume that you're just a failure and you'll never be able to heal.

Confrontation of perpetrators is especially likely to cause temporary setbacks. Every victim in our group who confronted her abuser had a setback after the event. Each victim became temporarily less functional, less strong in herself, and less motivated to heal. One dropped out of the group for a month. Another came to the group but wept for most of the hour. This is normal.

It's painful to break through the layers of denial and repression that usually surround abusive relationships. One woman said she felt as if she had a ten-ton weight on her chest for a week before and after the confrontation. Many victims temporarily regress to behaving like victims. But recovery comes more quickly afterward. Victims bounce back faster. They have learned to use their anger to their advantage, and they express it openly. They lean on friends during these times and journal their thoughts every day. They face depression again, but they know where the light is at the end of the tunnel.

Setbacks happen sometimes for no apparent reason at all. The road to recovery after abuse is not a smooth uphill glide. But remember, you are worth every effort.

Techniques for Handling Setbacks

1. Don't expect instant healing. Recognize that healing from abuse takes lots of time. Give yourself permission to take as much time as you need.

2. Don't expect perfection of yourself. Don't set yourself up for failure by expecting yourself to be the one woman in the world who will never have a setback.

3. Go with the flow. Allow your setback to happen. Don't fight it. Learn to experience it. Listen to what it tells you about yourself. Let it wash over you like a big wave. It will eventually wash out to

sea again. The more you fight it, the longer it will have to stay to force you to listen to it.

4. Listen to yourself. Listen to your inner being. Why are you having the setback? To what emotions, feelings, or memories is it tied?

5. Nurture yourself. As you go through this difficult time, be extra nice to yourself. Especially during your setbacks, treat yourself like royalty. Take a bubble bath. Say encouraging things to yourself.

6. Use your self-talk in positive ways; give yourself messages of hope. "You're going to make it just fine, kiddo, hang in there." "Every dark time means movement. Keep moving." "I may pass through these difficult waters again and again, but I'm willing to do it because I'm worth the effort!" "Every cloud has a silver lining." "I won't expect that perfection of myself that belongs only to God."

7. Keep your compass aimed at your own health and wholeness. Keep your eyes fixed upon the goal of your healing and happiness. A setback is only that—not the loss of hope or the end of healing.

8. Look for your trigger. What set you off this time? Was it being in the presence of your abuser? A TV program? A bad dream? Remembering something? A relationship problem? Identify the reason.

9. Look for clinical reasons for your flashback. See if you can figure out a function or a purpose for your setback. Why did it happen *now*? Is there a *message* that your unconscious is attempting to tell you? Are you possibly afraid to progress forward, and this setback is a covert way of stopping your own growth? Is there any deeper significance to your setback than that it just seemed to happen? Can you make a connection between your setback and any unfinished emotional business from your abuse? Learn to tie strong feelings to concrete issues from your abuse.

10. Remind yourself of the distance between what happened to you in your abuse and now. Keep reminding yourself, "That was then; this is now." "I was weak then; I am strong now." "I was a victim then; I am armed with the truth now."

11. If you have auditory or visual flashbacks, first make a safety plan so that if you fear losing control, you will know how to handle yourself. Then let the flashbacks happen. They're scary but OK.

When the flashbacks are over, give yourself permission to have them as often as your unconscious needs to send them to your consciousness. That way you can process what you need to remember or reexperience.

12. Learn to take your "garbage" out. Keep giving your pain to God. Remember it, forgive it, process it, and then give it to God.

13. Mentally construct a picture of yourself as completely whole. Then aim your life at that picture. Work at becoming that person, and don't give up until you have done so.

14. After the setback, get yourself back on track toward your continued healing. Don't allow the setback to win. You are in control now, not your past.

15. Learn that each time you have a setback and overcome it, you come away stronger than you were before. Little by little, you are getting stronger. Enjoy your strength.

16. Accept the fact that you would not be having a setback if you weren't growing and challenging your pain. So give yourself a pat on the back each time you have a setback. It represents forward progress, even if you feel that you're going full speed in reverse.

QUESTIONS FOR REFLECTION

1. In the first chapter you were encouraged to find two women friends to walk through your recovery with you. Assuming you have done this, have you told any other friends of your abuse? If so, what was it like to tell them? What feelings did you experience as you shared your story? If you have not shared with the two women friends or any others, why not? There are reasons. Do you know them?

2. What is (was) your darkest fear as you consider(ed) sharing what really happened to you?

3. How does ongoing secrecy keep a victim being a victim?

4. In a confrontation with a perpetrator, who has the most to lose: victim or perpetrator? Can you list three things that either may lose if silence is broken?

5. Many victims feel guilty about confronting their perpetrators. Why might a victim feel guilty about such a confrontation? Whose guilt is probably most operative in this situation?

═══ *ACTION ITEMS* ═══

1. If you were to confront your perpetrator, how would you do it? Would you write, make a phone call, confront in person, alone or with a friend, in front of others or privately? What would you say? Write your thoughts about this matter.

2. Show what you wrote (in your response to question 1) to a close female friend. Ask for her reactions.

FOR SPIRITUAL GROWTH

1. Read Matthew 18:15–17, and reflect upon the three stages of confrontation outlined in Scripture.

What is stage 1? _____

Stage 2? _____

Stage 3? _____

And if the perpetrator still chooses to live in his denial, what then?_____

Chapter 21

The
Last
Step

I was ecstatic! I had made it! It felt so good to be free and whole. And then I began to feel myself inexorably being drawn back into my life as a victim again. It didn't make sense.

The second time around I learned that I had not truly internalized what I thought I had learned. It had all been "head knowledge," and it needed to become "life-style" before I would be truly free.

That's why I decided to get involved with other women, to help them through their struggles—so that I myself could teach, practice, and become that which I had found to be so healing and wholesome.

People who have been deeply wounded in any way often wonder if they have to learn to live with a certain amount of residual effect of the wound. The answer is a qualified maybe. As one truly heals from deep wounds, the pain grows less. And as one learns healthy and productive means of relating to others, overcoming personal hurdles, and building positive self-esteem, life becomes not only bearable but enjoyable. Memories lose their power to evoke tears as they fade into becoming just part of one's history.

So it has been with a lady I'll call Connie. This book begins and ends with her story. Many times during the past few years she has asked, often through tears, if the struggle would ever end. I kept assuring her that as she kept working at conquering her dragons, life would indeed begin to soften and become more enjoyable.

During most of Connie's visits I would open the conversation by saying, "How are you doing, kiddo?" She would sigh deeply and say, "Well, I guess that's what I'm here to talk about." Her last visit was different. After my preliminary query she looked me straight in the eye and said, "I'm doing great! Things are really going well for me."

How does one grow from being a helpless victim to become a self-assured woman whose life and relationships are going well and who is very much in control of herself? Much of Connie's healing occurred as she committed part of her life to helping other victims overcome their pain. There is something very healing about working with people who are suffering as you once suffered. There is something very positive about taking the hand of a terrified and hopeless victim and leading her toward the path of her own healing.

There is also something very healing about being able to say to a woman, "I know what you're feeling. I have felt that way myself, and I'm here to tell you there is hope." And when that victim looks at you and says, "There may have been hope for you, but is there hope for me?" a victim has a triumphant feeling about being able to say, "Yes, my own life is a testimony to the fact that there is hope for you too."

Connie became one of the leaders in an ongoing ministry for female abuse victims. She has now worked with several such groups and has become quite an expert in helping women heal from their abuse. In the process of helping others, she found many landmarks on the path of her own healing.

She has actually stood before crowds of men and women and has said, "I am a sexual abuse victim. When I was a child I was sexually exploited by adult men. I'm here today to tell you a little about my story." If you're a victim, you might have trouble believing that a person could be bold enough to really go public with her story. There was a time when Connie would never have believed she could do it.

THREE STAGES OF HEALING

For victims of any kind there are three general stages of healing.

Stage 1

In this stage victims wade "through the swamp" to the first new feelings of wholeness and self-empowerment. This first stage is that of wading through the swamp, thrashing around for answers, agonizing with old feelings, going back for the "child," remembering, reuniting with a part of our self that we left behind, struggling long and hard, all the time focusing upon healing and wholeness. Toward the end of this stage the victim finally begins to feel that her feet have landed on somewhat solid ground.

This time can seem like an eternity. Victims frequently thrash, struggle, and agonize as they feel forever stuck in a hopeless quagmire. They vent anger at anyone who has the nerve to tell them that there may be hope and healing. They need for someone to walk beside them and encourage them as they journal their deepest memories, draw pictures to express their feelings, share memories of profound humiliation, recall (sometimes with terror) events that had been repressed, and struggle to make sense out of a life that has become confusing and chaotic.

Some try to "white knuckle" it through their healing alone, sharing with no one. Others use group therapy, individual therapy, pastoral counseling, and a network of women friends as much as possible. The latter group seems to heal far more rapidly than do the solitary victims, who usually don't get very far before they give up in hopelessness. Because they don't have the necessary support network behind them, they usually stumble and founder.

Somewhere along the way—and for some the way is much longer than for others—there begins to exist a dim glimmer of hope. Sometimes it's there for a fleeting moment and then gone as the darkness seems to surround them again. A month or two may pass before the glimmer returns, and then it may only be there briefly before the darkness again envelops the woman.

Time passes. The struggle continues. Slowly, slowly, the fleeting glimmer becomes a dim but steady glimmer. Then it becomes a little brighter. And one day the woman realizes that it has been several days since she last felt like a victim. It has been several days since her anger, fear, or sadness caused her to say or do something irrational. It has been several days since she used negative self-talk to make herself feel rotten about some small mistake.

That's the end of stage 1. Stage 1 is usually the hardest stage, with the deepest depression, the blackest black, and the most hopeless hopelessness. It is the stage in which a victim feels as if she will never be whole.

Stage 2

In stage 2 women reach out to one another, giving messages of hope and encouragement. Anger is used to help another victim believe she might have some grounds for being angry at her perpetrator. One victim's humiliation can motivate another victim to at least attempt to seek healing. In this stage one victim shows another what it can be like to express one's deepest feelings by doing so with her. One victim's tears are used to help wash the wounds of another's abuse.

Any leader knows that a teacher must know the subject better than the student. As one reaches out to help another, one is healed even more deeply.

However, you need to know that there is a potential trap in this process of trying to help others heal. The trap is that of believing you can do their work for them—that you can heal them if you pour enough of yourself into them.

Connie learned this lesson the hard way. In one of her groups there was a young woman we'll call Shannon. Shannon had been abused since she was a child, was still living in the home of her abuser, and was still being abused. Connie and Shannon hit it off almost immediately, and from that moment Shannon became Connie's project.

Connie poured herself into Shannon. Soon Shannon had moved in with Connie and was soaking up all of Connie's time and energy. Shannon was very needy—deservedly so after what she had been through—and Connie was very eager to do all she could for this victim.

The relationship lasted for several months. Connie gradually became less and less able to continue the relationship. She was getting worn out, drained, sucked dry. And she was starting to recognize that Shannon wasn't doing very much growing. There was overwhelming need in Shannon, but Connie didn't have the inexhaustible personal resources required to meet overwhelming need.

Finally a very difficult day came when Connie said, "I have a husband and children, and they're not getting very much from me these days. Shannon's getting it all. I'm so drained that I don't have much left to give to anyone." As we pondered her alternatives she realized that as much as it would hurt, Shannon had to go.

The decision was very painful for Connie, for she cared deeply for Shannon. But it was the right decision. From that point on Connie became a much more effective healer, because she learned that all she could do was to point the way toward healing. She could not walk the path for another victim. Healers can point the way and shout encouragement from the sideline, but victims are responsible for their own healing.

In stage 2, then, one uses all that she has learned about herself to help other victims—and there are plenty of victims to be helped. This is the stage of turning one's own pain and humiliation into a source of healing for other victims. It is the stage of deeper learning and deeper healing as one wades back into the swamp to help point the way to dry ground and wholeness.

During this stage the leader begins to accept her own limitations. She learns to establish and maintain appropriate boundaries, even with other victims. This lesson can be immensely freeing for a leader because she does not have to be superwoman. She learns that she can be herself, and that's enough.

Stage 3

The final stage is the one in which sexual abuse becomes almost a nonissue, for all the *right* reasons. One's life is no longer tied up in figuring out how to get through the swamp or in helping others get through the swamp.

At this final stage, life is just life. The abuse is no longer a repressed and hidden secret. It is a part of one's history, but it no longer controls every waking moment. And for the most part it doesn't hurt any longer.

Let's return to Connie's last visit, when she said that life was great. She also said that the time had come for her to take a break from working in our ministry for abuse victims.

Connie had some other personal goals for the next year or so. She had done her part in working with scores of women as a measure of offering thanks for her own healing. It was time to move back into the mainstream of life and to focus most of her energy upon her personal development, her husband, and her children.

Connie is a healed lady. She has reached stage 3. Her abuse is no longer the driving force in her life. By her own account, there are still moments in which she may recall some ugly memory, and there are times when she may still engage in negative self-talk. But she knows and daily practices the principles of wholeness in this book.

COMMENTS ON THE HEALING STAGES

Many victims identify stage 1 as their ultimate objective in healing. "If I could just get to the point of not feeling so rotten," they say. It's super to reach even stage 1, the most difficult and painful of all three stages.

The problem with reaching only stage 1 is that many victims then begin to backslide. They believe that having reached this stage, they will live happily ever after. Getting to stage 1 is like learning to use one computer program. But if that's all you learn, you'll soon forget it and will likely drift back into life as a victim. Moving from stage 1 through stage 2 is like becoming fluent in computer use. It becomes a way of doing life in general rather than just something more or less academically learned and forgotten.

In working with other victims (stage 2), one reinforces her own learning again and again. Her learning moves from head knowledge into the life-style. It becomes *part of you*; it becomes your personal vocabulary, your personal way of operating in all relationships. It becomes your way of thinking and processing. Not until it becomes who and what you are have you really *learned* the material. That's why stage 1 graduates often slip back into old patterns of behavior.

Stage 3 is significant in that it represents what most survivors thought they would experience at the end of stage 1: true freedom from the ongoing effects of abuse. It's the "free at last" stage, and it happens only after a woman has genuinely learned, practiced, and "become" all of the skills provided in this book. As wholeness becomes a way of life, pain and victimization naturally fade away. As one gives up practicing dysfunctional ways of living and relating to others in favor of learning how to function in healthy and productive ways, life becomes one's friend.

As one daily walks with God, God becomes a close friend. As one continually forgives, the load of unforgiveness lightens. As one learns to continually process her feelings, they eventually become her trusted allies. As one refuses to self-bash and continually feeds upon a diet of self-affirmation, she gains the ability to appreciate, accept, and love herself and others.

Stage 3, then, is the stage in which life has become so healthy, so natural, so peaceful, and so free that one is finally able to let go of her painful past and to focus upon her relationships and dreams. This stage comes naturally as a by-product of learning and practicing health.

In summary, stage 1 teaches how to process pain and outlines techniques and objectives of health. In stage 2 one practices what she is preaching. These elements (preaching and practicing) go hand in hand. Stage 3 is that of wholeness, in which a victim's life no longer needs to revolve around the issues of abuse.

I don't believe it's possible to leap from stage 1 to stage 3. If it is possible, I have not yet seen it. Some survivors find they need to walk through the swamp of stage 1 two or three times before they begin to feel that their feet are on solid ground. That's OK. Be patient with yourself as you heal. Go through the exercises in this book as often as you need in order to feel that you have made progress.

But don't stop after you have made some progress for yourself. Use what you have learned to reach out to other victims, or you will risk losing what you have learned. Become an advocate for other victims.

After you have helped other victims for a long enough time, you will begin to recognize the effects of health in yourself. The big picture will begin to make sense. Eventually, when you are sufficiently healed, you will find that you are able to move on comfortably with your life. Now your abuse is a part of your history rather than a dominant force.

QUESTIONS FOR REFLECTION

1. As you consider helping other women, what thought first comes to mind? Do you have concerns about your ability to truly help another woman? Do some journaling about what has been most helpful to you as you read through this book. Then speculate as to how you might use this knowledge to help others.

2. What is the trap inherent in helping other victims? How are you vulnerable to it, and how might you avoid it?

3. In which of the three stages would you say you are at this time? What clues lead you to believe you are in that stage?

═══ ACTION ITEMS ═══

1. If you are well into stage 1, then consider how you might find another woman who is a victim. Offer her your hand in friendship as you tell her about the healing path.

2. If you are not yet comfortable with the level of your own healing, then review the steps outlined in this book again. Study the book a second time. If you believe you are really stuck, then seek professional help.

3. Write a short story about a woman who was a victim and who finally reached stage 3. Who was she? How did she find healing? What did she encounter as she moved through stage 2?

FOR SPIRITUAL GROWTH

Memorize Hebrews 13:5, and make it your personal theme as you continue to walk with God.

Notes

Chapter 1

1. Scott Peck, *The Road Less Traveled* (New York: Touchstone, 1978), 15.

Chapter 3

1. *Harvard Mental Health Letter*, Feb. 1991, 1–2.
2. *Harvard Mental Health Letter*, Mar. 1991, 2.

Chapter 7

1. Michael Satchell with Gillian Sandford and René Riley, "Why the Secrets Slip Out," *U.S. News & World Report*, 1 June 1987, 21.
2. Ann Landers, "Adolescent Molester Needs a Close Watch," *St. Louis Post-Dispatch*, 1 November 1990, Living section.
3. Larry Corrigan, "New Family Realities Provide Increased Opportunity for Grandfathers to Sexually Abuse Toddlers," *Sexuality Today*, 9 November 1987, 3.

Chapter 8

1. Merle Fossum and Marilyn Mason, *Facing Shame: Families in Recovery* (New York: Norton, 1986), 143.
2. Maurine Moore and Donna Riekens, *Who Could I Tell: An Examination of Child Sex Abuse* (Dayton, Ohio: P.P.I. Publishing, 1985), 86.
3. Kee MacFarlane, Jill Waterman, Shawn Conerly, Linda Damon, Michael Durfee, and Suzanne Long, *Sexual Abuse of Young Children* (New York: Guilford Press, 1986).
4. Diane Broadhurst, *The Role of Law Enforcement in the Prevention and Treatment of Child Abuse and Neglect* (Washington, D.C.: Kirschner Associates, Inc., 1984).
5. Moore and Riekens, *Who Could I Tell*, 86.
6. MacFarlane and others, *Sexual Abuse of Young Children*, 206.
7. Fossum and Mason, *Facing Shame*, 142.
8. Claudia Black, *It Will Never Happen to Me!* (Denver: M.A.C. Publishers, 1981), 31–49.
9. Fossum and Mason, *Facing Shame*, 115.

Chapter 11

1. Reprinted and quoted by permission from New Harbinger Publications (Oakland, Calif.) from *When Anger Hurts, Quieting the Storm Within* (1989), Matthew McKay, Peter Rogers, and Judith McKay, 25–26.
2. Tim LaHaye and Bob Phillips, *Anger Is a Choice* (Grand Rapids: Zondervan, 1982), 36–38.

Chapter 12

1. McKay and others, *When Anger Hurts.*

Chapter 13

1. Fossum and Mason, *Facing Shame*, 39.

Chapter 14

1. Bruce Narramore, "Guilt: Christian Motivation or Neurotic Masochism," *Journal of Psychology and Theology*, vol. 2 (1974), 188.

Additional Resources

Bass, Ellen, and Laura Davis. *The Courage to Heal*. New York: Harper and Row, 1988.

Bradshaw, John. *Homecoming*. New York: Bantam Books, 1990.

Buhler, Rich. *Pain and Pretending*. Nashville, Tenn.: Thomas Nelson, 1988.

Freeman, Lucy, and Herbert Strean. *Guilt: Letting Go*. New York: John Wiley and Sons, 1986.

Gilligan, Carol. *In a Different Voice*. Cambridge, Mass.: Harvard University Press, 1982.

Jampolsky, Gerald, Patricia Hopkins, and William N. Thetford. *Goodbye to Guilt*. New York: Bantam Books, 1985.

Ledray, L. *Recovering from Rape*. New York: Henry Holt and Company, 1986.

McKay, Matthew, and Patrick Fanning. *Self-Esteem*. Oakland, Calif.: New Harbinger Publications, 1987.

Maltz, Wendy, and Beverly Holman. *Incest and Sexuality*. Lexington, Mass.: Lexington Books, 1987.

Missildine, Hugh. *Your Inner Child of the Past*. New York: Pocket Books, 1963.

Piaget, Jean. *The Moral Development of the Child*. New York: Macmillan, 1965.

Reed, Bobbie. *Pleasing You Is Destroying Me*. Waco: Word Books, 1992.

Sanford, Linda. *The Silent Children*. Garden City, New York: Anchor Press, 1980.

Solomon, Charles. *The Rejection Syndrome*. Wheaton, Ill.: Tyndale, 1983.

Splinter, John. *The Complete Divorce Recovery Handbook*. Grand Rapids: Zondervan, 1992.

Whitfield, Charles. *Healing the Child Within*. Deerfield Beach, Fla.: Health Communications, Inc., 1987.